The

FLAT

STICK

The FLAT STICK

The History, Romance, and Heartbreak of the Putter

Noah Liberman

Collins

An Imprint of HarperCollinsPublishers

HarperCollins books may be purchased for educational, business, or sales promotional use. For information please write: Special Markets Department, HarperCollins Publishers, 10 East 53rd Street, New York, NY 10022.

FIRST EDITION

Designed by William Ruoto

Library of Congress Cataloging-in-Publication Data has been applied for.

ISBN-13: 978-0-06-088743-8

ISBN-10: 0-06-088743-5

06 07 08 09 10 QW 9 8 7 6 5 4 3 2 1

For my dear family

CONTENTS

Acknowledgments

Writing a book means asking for myriad favors, large and small, and so I owe a debt of gratitude to many people who helped take me from novice to not-so-novice on the subject of putters. Putter designers David Mills, Bob Bettinardi, and Tad Moore were especially generous with their time and knowledge. Collectors and historians Jeffrey Ellis, David Levine, and Tim Janiga had much to tell me about the fascinating worlds of putter history and collecting. Ellis's stunning books, *The Golf Club* and *The Clubmaker's Art,* were sources not only of knowledge but of the gorgeous photographs of older clubs that fill chapter 3. Player representatives Giff Breed, Scott Sayers, Ed Kiernen, and Marc Player gave me access to their golfers and to the terrific stories they themselves have accumulated in their travels through the golf world. Industry publicists and friends Chris Smith, Larry Dorman, Barry Cronin, Meredith Geisler, Dan Shepherd, and K. DeKeyser, charming and helpful all of them, have been generous on more subjects than just putters over the years. Cliff Schrock, one of *Golf Digest*'s greatest resources, was likewise helpful to me, and Kim McCombs, a talented golf teacher and raconteur in Chicago, added to this project as he has many of mine. My editor at HarperCollins, Knox Huston, was a constant source of encouragement and good ideas, and designer William Ruoto put much effort into the lovely design of this book. Farley Chase and Scott Waxman of the Waxman Literary Agency did all the inscrutable things agents do for writers, always with skill and good humor. My deepest thanks goes to my family, who contributed to this book in every imaginable way.

Introduction

Most of us golfers love our putters for a round or two. Then we hate them. Recreational players, including the good ones, have a sense that the putter is a being unto itself—sometimes generous, often cruel, always capricious. Even professional golfers feel this, but they're loath to admit it. Pros are pros because they can control the game better than we can. But against the putter's stern authority, often they're as helpless as we are. "I'm having putting troubles, but it's not the putter, it's the puttee," a famous pro once said, suggesting that the golfer—the puttee—is just a pawn in this game. So what is this powerful being, the putter? And how does it derive this power? This book will answer those questions and more.

The putter is the club every golfer uses most, on nearly 40 percent of his shots. But it's the club that many recreational golfers practice with the least. It's the single club many golfers buy the most of—because it's the one they're most likely to grow disenchanted with. But it's also the rejected club most likely to be saved in the basement, just in case it feels just right again someday—because it will. It's the club whose visible design has changed the most in the past 25 years and that continues to inspire the most far-fetched innovations. Yet these innovations have led to scant improvement for pros—less than one shot per round. (And that's assuming it's not the lawn mower that should get the credit.) The putter is the club that generates the most euphoric highs and the most wretched lows. It's the club that offers the smallest margin for error and the club that betrays a golfer's weaknesses the most deeply—including those of his psyche. It's the club that gets broken most often over a knee.

You see, the putter is part of a relationship, between ourselves and it. But it has a privileged position from which to watch another relationship: the one between us and our inner selves. There's enlightenment and even some joy in studying all the ways golfers—we golfers—cultivate these relationships, then struggle to make them work. This book will be about these relationships.

The first book I wrote was about baseball gloves, and I realized as I was writing the book you're now reading that a glove and a putter are very different things.

You could say the glove embodies the sweet, uncomplicated attachments of childhood. But the putter embodies adulthood in all its fascinating complexity. As a grownup, you can't wake up without certain responsibilities, and as a golfer, you can't walk up to the first tee without a putter in your bag for when you eventually reach the green. But that's when the fun starts. So read on: you're away.

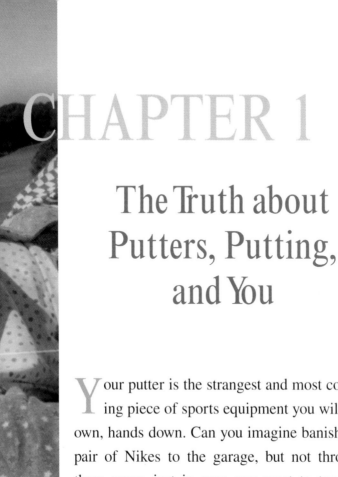

CHAPTER 1

The Truth about Putters, Putting, and You

Your putter is the strangest and most confusing piece of sports equipment you will ever own, hands down. Can you imagine banishing a pair of Nikes to the garage, but not throwing them away, just in case you want to try them again someday? How about buying several new baseball gloves every season and hoping one is magical? What if you blamed a missed layup on the basketball court and stuffed the ball in a trash can? Can you imagine heaving a bowling ball into a lake? Haven't you done all of those things to a putter? Wouldn't you like to right now?

If you're a golfer, you know that the putter

is a mysterious, vexing little object. But probably you've never had the courage to stare it in the face and figure out why. This book will help you do that. But in the process, you'll have to face certain facts about putters, and about putting, and about yourself, because the three are bound together the minute you step onto a green. Let's start by acknowledging a few truths.

TRUTH #1

PUTTING DOES NOT RESPOND TO OUR EFFORTS TO CONTROL IT

As a six-year-old, Tiger Woods was listening to subliminal tapes to improve his focus and self-control. As a 24-year-old—still a youngster by men's golf standards—he started a string of four consecutive major victories in which he simply didn't miss important putts under 10 feet. If this isn't focus and self-control, what is? Yet his then-coach, the respected Butch Harmon, was still bewildered. "One priority for Tiger—and I say this only half-jokingly—is to figure out why he putted so great in the majors this year," Harmon said. "And keep doing it, because it's the greatest putting under pressure I've ever seen." Clearly, neither man figured it out, because Woods now loses the occasional tournament with his putter and Harmon's no longer his coach.

The fact is, good putting comes and goes even in great putters, despite their attempts to coax it and keep it. "I play along every year waiting for one week, maybe two, when I can putt," said Larry Nelson, who for 25 years has been one of the very best putters in professional golf. It's no different for so-so putters. Chris Smith holds the record for the longest drive in tour history, 429 yards, and he admits he's not a great putter. (He was around 160th on the tour in putting in 2005, although he still mustered nearly $454,000 in earnings. Rough life.) The low point in his career came in an exhibition before the lowly Dakota Dunes Open of the Nike Tour in 1997. He was losing to Divot the Clown. As he said at the time, "It ticked me off because he wouldn't talk, and he had a horn on his nose and big shoes on. At that point, every fifty bucks you could pick up was important, and it was cash money, too. This Divot the Clown comes in and he's getting paid to do his exhibition show. He's in full clown garb and he's beating me. It was awful." But for Smith the long-driver, the finest moment of his career was on the greens during the final round of the Buick Classic, which he won, five years

Divot the Clown was the low point in PGA Tour pro Chris Smith's career. The high point came at the Buick Classic, where Smith knew every important putt was going in.

later. "It was just a day when I knew every putt I stood over was going in, every putt I needed to make," he says.

Smith just knew. But overall, golfers spend very little time knowing and a lot of time thinking and wondering. Which brings up this truth.

THE MORE YOU THINK, THE WORSE YOU GET

"*Happy Gilmore* is a pretty good instructional film," says PGA teaching pro Peter Donahue. He explains that the loopy Adam Sandler character has the most vital trait in a good putter: he's happy to putt. Donahue begins teaching his pupils by having them toss wadded-up paper balls into wastebaskets. "How much mental energy are you putting into this?" he asks. Almost none, of course, and the result is lots of nice tosses and that mindless pleasure humans get propelling stuff at targets. Donahue then counsels his pupils to bring this happy confidence to the putting green and never to lose it. This is a challenge. "Golfers train themselves not to love to shoot but to be afraid to miss," Donahue says. "It's like Red Auerbach said in basketball, 'I don't care if you miss, just don't be afraid to shoot.'" Donahue quotes statistics that show the best putters in the world are expert golfers like touring or teaching pros. The next-best putters are beginners. "And they're a lot better than everyone else in between," he says. "The reason is the innocence of their approach. They see it and they hit it. Experts are good because they've finally worked their way back to that simplicity."

If you want cruel proof of this, consider that the greatest putters always have loved to putt. "From the very beginning I enjoyed putting," said Ben Crenshaw in his autobiography. "I loved putting because it was just plain fun, and it fascinated me to watch the ball roll over those blades of grass. . . . And let's face it, sinking a putt is something all golfers enjoy." Okay, Ben. Gary Player was of this mind-set—or he convinced himself of it. In the spring, he'd talk of how much he loved putting on the grainy greens in the South. Later in the summer he'd say he loved putting on the slick bentgrass greens up North. Then he'd explain that he loved any green, "especially those I have to play today."

It's not just great putters who love a testy little task, though. Baseball Hall of Famer Brooks Robinson used to spend hours throwing a rubber ball against the cement steps in front of his childhood house and reacting to its bounces. Another Hall of Famer, Ozzie Smith, would lie on his back and toss a ball in the air and try to catch it while keeping his eyes closed. When you're wired like Ben and Brooks and Ozzie, you don't need to "work your way back to that simplicity." The rest of us do, and apparently that requires learning how to stop thinking. Meanwhile, here are two corollaries.

COROLLARY #1

"Putting is 90 percent mental. If you think you can't putt, you can't."

—FORMER PGA TOUR PRO GAY BREWER

COROLLARY #2

"The game of golf is 90 percent mental. The rest is mental."

—UBIQUITOUS

Wait a minute. If putting resists your efforts to control it and, in fact, the more you think about putting, the worse you do, then it's logical to conclude the following.

IT'S NOT YOUR FAULT WHEN YOU PUTT BADLY

The rational adult in you resists passing the buck this way, but the golfer in you does it anyway. All golfers, whether pros or hackers, never stop experimenting with new putters, new stances, new hand positions. Why? If the problem resides in something mechanical, it can't reside in your lack of skill. "When you can blame your poor performance on something external, it keeps you from being 'intra-punitive,' and it protects you from getting worse," says Larry Eimers, a sports psychologist who counsels pro golfers and has himself come within a stroke of qualifying for the U.S. Senior Open. What do pros do when they miss a putt? Frequently, they'll take a step toward the hole and tap down a "spike mark." "Guys do this all the time, and there's never a spike mark there," says Rob Burbick, a veteran club technician for Nike Golf who's fitted and adjusted clubs for pro golfers for more than a decade. (In fact, 75 percent of pros now use spikeless shoes, so there are almost no spike marks anyway.)

The best example of the "pass the buck" impulse comes, reassuringly, from Woods himself—when he was two years old. Already a phenom, little Tiger was on *The Mike Douglas Show,* squaring off against Bob Hope (no slouch himself) in a putting contest. After he'd missed three straight putts, Tiger complained that the putting green was not level. If little Tiger can pass the buck, so can you and I, right? Sure, up to a point. But adults are taught not to—which leads to this putting truth.

TRUTH #4

IT REALLY HELPS TO BE YOUNG

"I've been playing with my son Ryan, and he's such a good putter," said Australian pro Craig Parry a few years ago. "When I had my putts for par to save, I thought, 'Just do what Ryan would do—right speed and in the middle of the hole.' There's no thought of missing it because he's so new to the game."

Woods was 21 when he holed every single putt he had from under 10 feet on his way to a mind-boggling 12-stroke victory in the 1997 Masters, a performance many consider the greatest ever. He was 24 when he won

IT'S HARD FOR THEM, TOO

PGA Tour pros make 99 percent or more of their putts from two feet or closer, right? Nope. They miss at least six out of every 100—an astonishingly high number. They make roughly one-third of their putts from twenty feet, right? No again: they make no more than one in six. As if the truth of putting weren't hard enough, we make things worse by imagining it's easier for the pros than it is.

the 2000 PGA Championship. On the 16th green that Sunday, he got his 20-foot birdie putt rolling, then started stalking the ball, pointing at it and ordering it into the hole. It went in and helped Woods get into a playoff with Bob May, which he won.

Fast-forward five years: Woods isn't putting like a kid anymore. We remember his stunning chip-in on the 70th hole of the 2005 Masters but tend to forget that he bogeyed the next two holes, making a play-off necessary. At the U.S. Open, he bogeyed the 70th and 71st

At the 2005 U.S. Open, putting bewildered Tiger. Five years earlier, his brilliant putting bewildered even his coach, Butch Harmon.

holes to lose by two strokes. He was first in greens in regulation that week but finished next to last in putting. "Unfortunately, it's frustrating," he said. "If I just putt normal, I'm looking pretty good."

In 2001, Harmon wondered how Tiger putted so well. In 2005, Tiger wondered why he couldn't. Age is one reason. It's a story told a thousand times in pro golf—the older a player gets, the more susceptible he or she is to the effects of fear and self-consciousness. A fearless, charging putter like Arnold Palmer became timid and inconsistent toward the end of his competitive days. A brilliant, intuitive "feel" putter like Ben Crenshaw fought to find his touch later in his PGA Tour career. Crenshaw wrote something about Tiger in his 2001 autobiography that says it all: "His stroke is very authoritative, which it should be at that age."

It's not just golfers who benefit from youthful courage. Gymnasts and figure skaters—especially women—often peak in their late teens partly for physical reasons but also because they're not mature enough emotionally to suffer the psychological contortions that plague us adults. Young golfers don't overthink a four-footer because missing it isn't loaded with awful connotations. And as if putting weren't scary enough, there's this ironic little truth.

THE SHORTER THE PUTT, THE MORE NERVOUS YOU GET

A testy short putt: It counts as much on the scorecard as a booming drive, yet when it's off by so much as a quarter inch, it can demolish a round faster than a long slice into the woods. Why? Again, your psyche, which goes into overdrive near the cup. "You're in a risk area where you're liable to suffer humiliation or embarrassment if you miss it," Eimers says. "Everyone hates this putt, because if you make it, no one gives a damn, but if you miss it, everyone raises their eyebrows. In the end, you're working 18 holes to avoid humiliation." That's a lot of baggage, but the shot can define a round—or a career. As one former pro told Eimers, "If you're going to make it up here, you have to make every four-footer." I did say *former* pro.

Not content to burden us with just humiliation and embarrassment, Eimers delivers the whole emotional enchilada. "Putting is probably the most exquisite representation of your inner emotional state," he says. "If you don't feel you deserve to make a putt, it will show up in a tiny twitch or a little pause—and you won't make that putt."

Heavy stuff. So here's something a little wacky.

THERE'S SOMETHING FRIGHTENING ABOUT THE FOUR-FOOTER SPECIFICALLY

Not the three-footer, or even the five-footer, although it is, you know, longer. The four-footer is the archetypal knee-knocker. It's what golfers talk about when they're discussing fear. Billy Casper used to say, "Practice four-footers twice as much as you practice the long ones." He knew what was at stake.

When Colin Montgomerie mentions four-footers, he also mentions his failed marriage. "In those days [before his recent putting problems], my ex-wife used to walk to the next tee when I had a four-footer because I never missed. Now that wouldn't happen, firstly because she's not there anymore and secondly because [I'm] all a bit sweaty over the short ones." So four-footers are freaky, and this leads to several corollaries.

Colin Montgomerie used to be steady on the four-footers; now he's "all a bit sweaty" over them.

If you're sticking your 6-iron to four feet, well,
you'd better practice your 6-iron more.

If you're lagging putts to four feet, you might as
well start charging 'em.

»» COMIC BOOKS: «
LEARNING HOW TO PUTT

There are roughly a million how-to-putt books out
there. The how-to-putt bible is, well, *Dave Pelz's
Putting Bible*. This is a 400-page work, and it's
amazing, as bibles are supposed to be. And like a
bible, it's stuffed cover-to-cover with information
that's profound, or arcane, or sometimes even
downright trivial. Pelz's bible is also out of its mind.
On page 341, Pelz has a section called "Polish Your

Attitude," where he writes, "Here comes what is, for many, the hard part." It only took him 341 pages to get to the hard part of putting? On page 262 you'll find subchapter 11.7, "How to Aim." Isn't this like finding Adam and Eve somewhere back in the book of Ezekiel? But apparently there's a lot to learn before how to aim, like the information in Figure 9.10.1, which illustrates the following: "If contacted on a foot, a ball with feet would roll more oddly than a football."

How-to-putt books are monuments to hope and proof of the naïveté that's necessary if you're going to pick up a putter and actually hope. For each one, there's an author who thinks he or she has figured out putting, and at least one reader who thinks he or she can digest the result and remember it on the golf course the next day. It's really quite adorable.

PGA teaching pro Todd Sones starts his attempt, *Lights-Out Putting,* with the chapter "Attitude Is Everything." The "traits of a great putting attitude," he says, are Greatness, Confidence, Decisiveness, Imagination, Responsibility and Awareness, Fear, and Effort. The nice thing about *Lights-Out Putting* is that even if you don't master putting, you'll probably be able to tell your therapist you've outgrown him.

It's easy to poke fun at how-to-putt books, because putting is, by its very nature, absurd. So you have to credit Pelz and Sones—both star teachers— for facing the challenge head-on. And you really have to respect their intentions, because a person must have real empathy for the human condition even to think of writing a how-to-putt book.

But that doesn't prevent the results from often being as absurd as putting itself. For example, on page 294, Pelz offers a drill to keep you from moving your head while you putt. In the drill, you address a ball with your hair barely grazing a wall. If you move your head during the stroke, you'll feel the wall against your hair. Cool. But what if you have no hair?

Now that we've introduced a little weirdness to the mix, let's add more, courtesy of putting guru Dave Pelz. In his voluminous writings, Pelz has explained myriad truths, including:

> Our *body* is not to be trusted: If you find a putting stroke that feels comfortable and "natural," it's likely to lead to disaster. Also, you must not do "whatever feels right to you," because it won't necessarily produce an accurate, repeatable stroke.

> Our *eyes* are not to be trusted: We typically read only 30 percent of the real break on a putt. But we learn to compensate, subconsciously, and manage to aim for 65 to 75 percent of the break. Then we make up *some* of the remaining shortfall in the stroke itself. Pelz writes, "In golf, the subconscious always wins." Except that we're still underplaying the stupid break, missing up to 90 percent of our putts below the hole. Even pros miss up to 80 percent below!

> Not even our *words* can be trusted: When we aim for a spot an inch outside the cup, we're playing 3⅛ inches of break (from the center of the cup). But we call it "an inch of break."

> Until these built-in defects of ours (and dozens of others) are eradicated, practicing is generally worthless—or worse. One in ten golfers gets better

through practicing, four stay the same, and five get worse, Pelz writes.

❯ Now, once we've eradicated the flaws in our bodies, our senses, and even our native tongue, we must practice the right way—a lot. It takes 100 repetitions to form a proper habit, according to Pelz, and 10,000 to "ingrain and own it." Ten thousand repetitions? Who would have time to take out the trash? Besides which, there is this harsh truth.

TRUTH #7

RELATIVE TO ITS IMPORTANCE TO YOUR SCORE, PUTTING IS WHAT YOU PRACTICE THE LEAST

At every level of play, putting comprises more than 40 percent of the game of golf. Its importance is reflected in something the great golfer and course architect Willie Park used to say: "A man who can putt is a match for anyone, and a man who cannot is a match for no one." Evidence: in 1999, out of 11 majors contested in the three top U.S. tours, eight of the winners ranked eighth or better in putting that week; at the U.S. Open in 2004, 11 of the top 15 long-drivers missed the cut, but only one of the top 14 putters did. And teaching pro Todd Sones writes in *Lights-Out Putting*, "The putting/performance relationship holds true for the amateur ranks as well, with one exception: it's more severe." He goes on to say, "Believing that holing a putt is just as rewarding as nailing a 275-yard drive right down the heart of the fairway is a major step toward developing a great putting attitude." Trouble is, many golfers don't want to believe this, and one of the reasons is that many golfers hate to practice putting. Pelz has said that while putting makes up 40 percent of our strokes, it makes up "80 percent of the anguish." Does putting make up 40 percent of your practice time? The last time you had an hour to practice, didn't you beat balls on the driving range? Even the generic term for practicing, "beating balls," derives from the range, not the green. Practicing putting involves both anguish and drudgery—unless you're a nutty genius like Crenshaw. Champions Tour member Jim Thorpe recalled a big decision he had to make. "[On Wednesday] I was on the putting green thinking, 'Should I stay here and work on my putting or should I go play blackjack?' I stayed and putted." And that week,

KEEP YOUR HEAD

University of Virginia golf coach Bowen Sargent used to play minor tour events with current PGA Tour players Chris Riley and Chad Campbell, and one day Campbell told him, "Nobody has seen anybody putt like Chris Riley." So Sargent asked Riley for his secret, and Riley demurred. "I don't know you that well," he said, according to Todd Ciuba, Riley's agent for SFX sports group. Sargent continued to struggle with his putting, so he kept after Riley. Finally, Riley agreed to divulge the secret, and Sargent expected an epiphany. "Keep your head down," Riley stated. "That's it. That's all I think about." Sargent tried it for a week—and putted worse!

he won the Charles Schwab Cup Championship, setting 18-, 36-, and 72-hole scoring records.

RELATIVE TO ITS IMPORTANCE, PUTTING IS THE PART OF THE GAME WE REMEMBER THE LEAST

Golf Digest's John Hawkins flushed this one: "It's not uncommon to hear a tour player bemoan a low score that got away by saying, 'I played great but didn't make anything,' as if putting doesn't actually factor into the quality of a round. That's like declaring the three-hour drive from grandma's house a huge success despite the guardrail you took out five miles from home." If you've never weaseled out this way, you've never golfed. But here's more fascinating proof of Hawkins's point. In a terrific book called *My Greatest Shot*, 100 pro golfers are quoted in response to a letter sent by a golf-crazy dentist, Ron Cherney. Remember, 40 percent of golf is putting. Yet only 10 of the 100 golfers identify a putt as their greatest shot. (Interestingly, of the 10 women pros who responded, five named a putt.) Jack Nicklaus never tires of talking about golf and Jack Nicklaus—which is fine, because he's probably the smartest golfer ever. So it's not surprising that Jack describes not one but eight shots, and it's reassuring that two of them are putts. Nicklaus, a great putter, knows how important putting is.

But why have putts registered with so few of the 100? Why, in fact, have 89 of the remaining 90 identified an iron shot of one sort or another when such shots represent only slightly more of the typical round than putts do? Perhaps iron shots just grab our imagination more. They are the most varied, from full-strength 240-yarders to feathery 10-yarders. They certainly are pivotal shots, in that they set up putts and often must make up for poor drives. In this respect, they can mean a swing of two or more shots on a hole. They also tend to involve the most varied shotmaking—draws, fades, chips, pitches, and so on—around the most challenging impediments: trees, traps, and lakes. Refining the equation, long iron shots are the single-most-identified shot among the 100, even though they make up much less of every round than putts, short irons, and drives. Woods has holed dozens of colossal putts, but his "greatest" shot was an uphill 200-yard iron from a fairway bunker on the 18th at Hazeltine in the 2002 PGA Championship. "I felt like I was looking at a bogey and somehow turned it into a three." Interestingly, this wasn't the final hole of the tournament, and Woods didn't win the event anyway. The shot was relatively meaningless, but to Tiger, it represented the greatest combination of difficulty, skill, and scoring payoff in his life. It's a very rational, clinical answer from perhaps the most dramatic golfer ever—the one who ordered a putt into the hole and whose post-putt fist-pump is his signature. Somehow, even Tiger wants to disregard his putts.

Now, there's a very compelling truth (at least in my book) that might account for much of what's vexed us so far—for why we don't practice putting as we should, for why we're ashamed to miss putts, for why we won't even acknowledge how important putting is. But this truth is pretty heavy.

TRUTH #9

WE ARE GENETICALLY ENCODED TO FEAR PUTTING

Stick with me on this one, even though you're just dying to go putt. Social anthropology has shown that humans have two favorite landscapes: the kind they lived in as adolescents and, even more so, a grassy parkland. Richard Conniff in *Discover* magazine described the latter as "landscapes with open, grassy vegetation, scattered strands of branchy trees, water, changes in elevation, winding trails and brightly lit clearings . . ." (Sounds like a golf course!) Harvard biologist Edward O. Wilson, author of the famous 1975 book *Sociobiology,* once said, "I believe that the reason that people find well-landscaped golf courses 'beautiful' is that they look like savannas, down to the scattered trees, copses and lakes, and most especially if they have vistas of the sea." (Sounds like Harbour Town!)

For our hunting ancestors, the woods provided cover, the expanses were where they could spot prey, and the low-lying water was likely to draw even more prey. They especially liked being able to peer down on the animals. As Steve Sailer wrote in the *American Conservative* on the golf-course architecture revival, "Our ancestors would study the direction of the wind and the slopes of the land in order to approach their prey from the best angles." It all relates, say the experts, to an essential question animals ask themselves: Should I explore or should I flee? (Should I lay up or go for the green? Sounds like course management!) The thinkers have suggested why we—especially hunting-bred males—like golf. But they haven't gone far enough. They've explained why we like hitting powerful drives and dramatic iron shots, but they haven't explained why we get wiggier as we get toward the green and why putting involves so many of the neuroses that the long game doesn't. Here's why: when we're on the green, we're no longer the hunter—we're the hunted. Gone are the commanding vistas and the trees for cover. Gone is the

Is this the Harbour Town Golf Links, or the ideal landscape for the genetically encoded hunter in all of us?

Courtesy of The Sea Pines Resort

long-range weapon, like a driver, and in its place is a putter. And we're alone and vulnerable at (often) the lowest spot on the hole.

This is good news, people. It means we putters are not to blame for being ineffectual, compulsive, self-reproaching, self-evading, forgetful slobs who get worse as we grow older. Because we're really not putting at all. Our genetic ancestry is. And it's lousy.

And this nicely explains a surprising truth about putting.

PUTTING ISN'T EVEN GOLF

Current PGA Tour pro Peter Jacobsen and his family didn't bother to putt when they played golf during his childhood. This allowed them to play more holes. Jack Fleck, a contemporary of Ben Hogan's, said he could have had a better career if he hadn't had to putt. "I've always thought too much of a premium was put on putting," he said. "A putt hangs on the lip and you hit it a quarter of an inch and that's equal to a good drive or a good wedge." Fleck felt a putt should count for only half a stroke. An-

GENETICS, PART TWO

If you buy my claim that we're genetically encoded to fear putting, then you might also agree that genetics can play a role in your stroke, once you've worked up the courage to walk onto the green. Basically, it helps to be born with "touch." "Doctors make good putters. They know how to be delicate with their hands," says Kim McCombs, a Chicago golf teacher for more than 30 years. "Plumbers are lousy putters. I've taught some plumbers, and they have amazingly strong hands. They can use their wrists to slap the ball 250 yards on a line, sometimes. But they can't putt.

"I've had some jazz guitarists who could really putt," he adds. You don't get to be a surgeon (at least a good one) or a jazz musician without innate touch. And I daresay if you gravitated into plumbing and into bad putting, you wouldn't have made a good surgeon, even though you might be brilliant.

And as McCombs sees it, small hands and short arms make for better putters. The smaller hands make for a more intimate relationship with the grip. Shorter arms are easier to control, easier to "groove." "You look at a lot of the great putters, they have small hands," McCombs says. "Tiger Woods has small hands, especially for such a large man. Jack Nicklaus has tiny hands. In his book, *Golf My Way*, there's an outline sketch of his hand. His fingers barely reach my first knuckle. [McCombs is not a great putter himself, he admits. But he is long off the tee.] If I walked in a room and had to pick out the best putter, I'd go right for the guy who's built like Jack Nicklaus, with those small hands and those short arms."

nika Sorenstam is the greatest woman golfer ever, and it blows experts' minds to imagine how good she'd be if she could really putt. Hogan wasn't a great putter, either, and he rued it. "There is no similarity between golf and putting," he argued. "They are two different games, one played in the air, the other on the ground."

If putting isn't even golf, then it's no stretch to acknowledge our final truth. This one brings us back to the putter itself and reinforces Truth #1, that putting resists our efforts to control it.

THE PUTTER IS A BEING
UNTO ITSELF

"I'm having putting troubles, but it's not the putter, it's the puttee," pro Frank Beard once said, implying that the golfer is controlled by the club, not the other way around. Sergio Garcia understands this. At the 1999 Irish Open, the 19-year-old Garcia holed a putt from 30 feet on the first hole, from 35 on the sixth, 45 on the 12th, and 35 on the 13th. He won the event by three strokes, sinking a birdie putt on the 18th for good measure. "I have never putted like that in my life," he effused afterward. *"My putter was crazy."*

Former pro golfer Kel Devlin—the son of former PGA Tour star Bruce Devlin—tells a funny story from his own days on the satellite tours. His playing partner walked off the 18th green and his caddy asked him if he wanted his clubs stored for the night. He said yes, except for his putter. "I'm taking it home with me," he said. The caddy asked why. "I'm putting it in the toilet," he answered. *"I want it to be with the rest of its friends."*

Understand now?

CHAPTER 2

Great Putting Performances

(and the Putters That Made Them Happen)

For every great putting performance there's a putter, let's not forget. So before we go any further into our study of the flat stick—and just in case chapter 1 made you wonder why you even bother to walk onto a green—let me treat you to a handful of stories about great putts. And about great putting rounds, tournaments, and seasons. You might remember some of these performances; in some cases, they defined a career. But even if they're new to you, you'll understand the great things a golfer really can achieve with a putter. To this end, we'll look closely at the flat sticks themselves, along with the great putts.

TWO BLACK KNIGHTS

When a player comes from six strokes behind on the final day to win the Masters by one stroke, it's hard to single out one of his shots as the greatest. Gary Player took 64 strokes to finish Augusta National on an April Sunday in 1978—at that time the tournament record—making dozens of excellent shots with little margin for error. But he'll tell you the greatest one was his final putt, a downhill 16-footer with a little bit of left-to-right break, that split the hole in half. The putt capped a 30 on the back nine, and since there were several groups behind Player, he could only guess at how important that putt was. As it turned out, three players finished one stroke behind him. So there was an air of grateful relief when he described

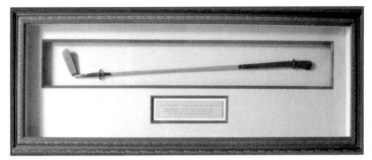

The Black Knight's Black Knight.

the putt several years later. "I say my prayers every day of my life, and I say thank you for many things—my health, my family, and for the talent that has been loaned to me, and it is then that I always think of that putt going in at 18. It's the most significant thing that has ever happened to me. That putt at Augusta, that was the single best shot of my career," Player said. Many things, in retrospect, must add to the glow of that shot for Player. The win was his third at Augusta, and it was also the final of his nine wins in major championships. But others savored the moment, as well. His playing partner was a young Seve Ballesteros, who was wrapping up a disappointing 74. How like the Spaniard, who has always found ways to wring the most out of every great moment on the course, to revel in Player's putt. He rushed across the green and gave Player a huge hug.

The putter in Player's hands at that moment was the same one he used for more than 100 wins worldwide, and everything about it will sound quaint today, in an era of heavily marketed putter brands and players demanding minute, high-tech tweaks. Player found his putter in a barrel full of odd putters and wedges in a golf shop in the famous Ginza shopping area of Tokyo, where he was browsing with Arnold Palmer. The shopkeeper noted Player's interest—and marked the stick up to 55 yen, from 5, before Player returned to buy it. The putter had no brand name; it was just a simple black blade. Over the years, Player added some layers of lead tape to the head, and he always kept a can of black spray paint handy to touch up the head and the hosel. The putter was known as the Black Knight, just like Player himself, when the man was contending in top events. But in the years after, Player began referring to it as Old Faithful. It forms part of the 300-piece memorabilia collection that Player had on the market as this book was being written.

BARBERED

Jerry Barber's name doesn't always come up when people are listing the greatest putters ever, but it should. Maybe he was just a little too irritating on the green for folks to remember his putting warmly. Barber was a slow player who took forever over putts, demanded that his playing partners use pennies to mark their balls because he said dimes distracted him, and sometimes rankled opponents with gamesmanship on the green that bordered on bad sportsmanship. But players who paid attention to Barber saw a tireless practice player, a serious student of the game, a generous (though stubborn) teacher, and a warm-hearted guy. He was a short-game wizard who pioneered the use of the sand wedge as a lob wedge, and his aggressive, wristy putting stroke was straight out of an earlier era. The putter he used to win the 1961 PGA—well, it was straight out of his workshop: a simple brass-head, heel-shafted Fred Matzie blade with a startlingly upright lie angle and a wad of lead tape added to the end, apparently to maintain line and pace during his aggressive stroke. Lee Trevino said it was the heaviest putter he'd ever felt.

Barber had three aggressive birdie putts to finish the fourth round of the 1961 PGA Championship. He started the 16th hole four strokes back of Don January. On the 16th, he curled in a 25-footer for birdie. On the 17th hole, it was a 40-footer. On the 18th, he rammed home a 60-footer that had two distinct breaks. Accounts say he played four feet of break, but he was quoted saying it was eight, left to right. Regardless, January played in at one-over, and suddenly he was in a Monday play-off with the pesky Barber, who continued putting splendidly and so irritated January with his slow play that January complained to officials. Barber eventually won—his only major championship victory. The duffers among us will appreciate this fact: Barber reached the play-off despite hitting two of his drives on Sunday less than 100 yards— proof of the importance of putting and validation of Barber's own axiom: The harder I practice, the luckier I get.

THANKS, CHRIS CHAPMAN

Many great players make a quest of collecting the clubs they used to win major tournaments, and can you blame them? But Tom Watson isn't one of them, apparently, and his lack of interest extends to his putters, even though he's one of the greatest ever on the greens. Several of Watson's putting performances would make any "Top" list, including a 20-footer he nailed on the 72nd hole at Carnoustie in 1975 to force an 18-hole play-off, in which he beat Jack Newton by one stroke. "I almost strained my arm pumping the air," he later said of his celebration. You could add the 60-footer he made two years later at Turnberry to catch Jack Nicklaus on the 69th hole of the 1977 British Open, where he birdied the last two holes to beat Nicklaus by one stroke. And just for kicks, you could toss in his 2002 U.S. Senior Open performance, where he birdied 6 of the last 10 holes to force a play-off with Don Pooley.

The putters? Watson used a Ping Anser in the 1975 British—as so many of his peers were doing. He used a Wilson 8813 blade in the 1977 tournament—a version of Wilson's 8802 and a distinctly more demanding putter than the heel-toe-balanced Anser. So where is the Ping today? "No idea what happened to it," Watson says. The Wilson?

Jack Nicklaus congratulated Tom Watson after Watson beat him dramatically in the 1977 British Open; a few months later, Watson returned this Wilson 8813 putter to the youngster he'd borrowed it from back home.

Brian Morgan/Getty Images

"I returned [it] to the kid who gave it to me, Chris Chapman." Kid? And who's Chris Chapman? "Chris at that time was a youngster at the club where I played most of my golf, the Kansas City Country Club," Watson says. "I borrowed the putter, used it only a few months, then Chris asked for it back." Watson obliged. And what about the putter he used at the 2002 Senior Open? "I can't recall the putter I used at this time," Watson says. The Senior Open loss was bitter for Watson, who had suffered a string of second-place finishes and said at the time that he was feeling "like Phil Mickelson to Tiger Woods." It couldn't have helped that Pooley iced the tournament with a nine-foot birdie putt, the kind Watson had sunk to force the play-off. So maybe that's why he can't remember his putter that day, and maybe some sympathetic reader will remind him. Here's hoping, as well, that someone has located the Anser from 1975 and that Chris Chapman is taking good care of the 8813 that served Watson so well three decades ago.

GOOD EXERCISE

Larry Nelson went for a little jog one morning in 1983. He was tied with Watson for the lead in the U.S. Open with three holes to play when he left himself with a 60-foot birdie putt on the testy par-3 16th at Oakmont. "I remember it like it was yesterday," he told *Golf World UK* a decade later. "Despite the rain, the greens were really quick. They had been cut again that morning, and this putt was a little downhill and also down the grain. . . . To get the ball within ten feet of the hole would have been good." In fact, something else happened at that distance: "Those greens were so true that I knew the ball was in when it was 10 feet away." Seconds later, Nelson broke into his celebratory jog, then went on to win the tournament by one stroke. The putter he was using that day was a Ping B60 prototype he'd received from a company rep. The B60 of that era was one of the more graceful Pings—heel-toe-weighted and with a gooseneck, of course, but with a gently fluted, rounded flange instead of the squared-off angles of the Anser and others. It was the putter Nelson used to win the 1981 PGA Championship, as well, and he retired it in 1986, he says. This was a long time for Nelson to stick with a club; he's famous for having used three sets of irons in four rounds when he won the 1987 PGA Championship. "They all looked so good, they all deserved a chance," Nelson quipped.

UNSENTIMENTAL AND UNBEATABLE

You can win a tournament with one putt, if it's dramatic enough. Or you can win one with 114, as Billy Casper did the 1959 U.S. Open at Winged Foot. Casper had 31 one-putts that week, almost one every other hole. At one point he had nine straight one-putt greens. It was just his fourth year on the tour, and he hadn't qualified for the Masters earlier in the season, so he felt a good showing at the U.S. Open was crucial. His putter helped him get back on track. It was a Golfcraft Caliente, a smallish mallet with a fiberglass shaft, three spaced dots indicating the sweet spot and aimline, and a modest offset. Casper was known as a deadly serious competitor and superior tactician who didn't go in for Trevino-like humor and often got angry with himself on the course. Dave Marr described him this way many years ago: "Billy was just a killer on the golf course. He just gave you this terrible feeling he was never going to make a mistake, and then of course he'd drive that stake through your heart with that putter. It was a very efficient operation."

Casper's efficiency seems to include an unsentimental approach to his putters themselves. He gave the Caliente to the USGA's Golf House shortly after the win. "Billy wasn't particularly close or tight with that putter, although it did help usher in the popularity of mallet-head putters," explained a publicist for Billy Casper Golf recently. When reminded that some players get quite attached to putters, especially ones they used to win majors, Casper's publicist added, "Billy doesn't have much more to say about putters in general, because ironically, he's not a putter geek." He's never had to be.

INTRODUCING BOB BRUE

Here's a name you don't read every day in "Greatest" lists. Bob Brue never had a PGA Tour win, but he amassed more than $1 million in earnings in a long career, despite playing much of it when the money was modest. "I was second in the Phoenix Open in 1964, which Jack Nicklaus won. You know how much I made? Four thousand dollars. Now a guy wins hundreds of thousands for that," Brue says. But not with bitterness. Brue is a jovial man whose retirement hobby is entertaining crowds with a trick-shot and comedy routine. "Where do they get the seeds for seedless grapes?" he quips. "Whatever happened to Absorbine Sr.?"

Well, he was plenty loose at the Senior Tour's Kroger Classic in 1994: he had just 17 in all in the second round, a tour record. Putting wasn't Brue's strong suit—it was mid-irons, he says—but on that day he put everything together, hitting lots of irons close to the pin and draining a lot of 8-to-10-footers. But that still doesn't explain an average of one putt per hole. Small greens and lots of one-putts from the fringe do explain it: they count as no-putts. "That course had a lot of really small greens and pins tucked near the collars," Brue says. "I was on a lot of collars, pretty close to a lot of pins." He finished the day with a 35-foot no-putt from the fringe, to shoot a 66. "I remember very distinctly playing with Jim Dent that day. He's a really fast player and I'm a really deliberate player. When I sank that one for birdie, he wasn't mad, he just couldn't believe what was going on. When we totaled it up, I was afraid they wouldn't give me credit for it."

Brue's putter that day was a Ping JB5, a more face-balanced kin to the B60 described earlier with Larry Nelson. It was 40 or 42 inches long, Brue says, because he'd developed a grip that put the hands a good six inches apart, to take the wrists out of the stroke. He sees it as a precursor to the long putters of today. "We didn't know about sticking the putter into your belly back then, but this way worked for me."

THE FAX DAY'S HISTORIC SEASON

No one has putted better over a whole season than Brad Faxon, according to the PGA Tour record book. In 2000, he averaged 1.704 putts per green in regulation—that's the equivalent of a birdie putt on 30 percent of the holes he played. The putter he used that season, and every season since, is a Scotty Cameron prototype made similar to the Ping My Day that Faxon used before he became a

Cameron devotee. He and Cameron call his current putter the "Fax Day," as Cameron likes to nod to the Ping designs that he has modified with slight adjustments in weighting, materials, and finish. One of his models is called the Scottydale, a pun on Scottsdale, where some of the earliest and most sought-after Pings were made by designer and founder Karsten Solheim.

Faxon's Fax Day is a dark brown–tinted stainless steel. All Cameron did for Faxon during the 2000 season was adjust the loft a little bit and change the grips a couple of times, Faxon says. But even a grip change is a meticulous matter for Faxon, who often has Cameron put a few on before he finds one that feels just right in his hands. Nevertheless, he rejects the notion that he's got a "Princess and the Pea" approach to putters. "That's inaccurate. Once I get it where I want it, I just don't want to mess with it," he says.

He remembers putting well in 2000, but he also remembers starting the following year with a bang, winning the season's third event, the Sony Open, with a 20-under 260. He eagled four of the eight par-5s that week, and that included an eight-footer on the 72nd hole, when he already had the tournament sewn up. "It lined up just outside the left edge of the cup, and it was the purest stroke, the purest feeling I've ever had over a putt to this day. My hands felt soft, the putter head felt heavy, the contact was dead center and the ball went into the middle of the cup. My caddy said it would have gone into a thimble."

STILL NO RESPONSE

When *Golf World UK* surveyed the long history of golf in 1992 and came up with the 20 greatest putts to that date, it chose 3 of Jack Nicklaus's: a 30-footer on the 16th at Augusta to tighten the noose on Johnny Miller and Tom Weiskopf in the final round of the 1975 Masters, one of the greatest showdowns ever; a 30-footer he nailed on the final hole of the 1977 British Open at Turnberry to force Tom Watson to make his two-footer for the win; and the S-curve 11-footer he made on the 71st hole of the 1986 Masters to steal the lead for good from Seve Ballesteros on the way to a 30 on the back nine.

Now, if you're looking for wacky stories about Nicklaus's putters on those precise three days, you're not going to get them. For the two British Open wins, he was using the George Low Wizard 600 flanged blade that accompanied him for 15 of his 18 major wins. (For a picture of that classic heel-shafted putter, see page 81.) For the third, he used a MacGregor Response MI 615—an enormous center-shafted, heel-toe-balanced stick that

David Cannon/Getty Images

Courtesy of Chris Smith

Jack Nicklaus exults after his world-beating birdie at the 1986 Masters. Cameron Smith exults a decade later, thinking his dad had found the putter Nicklaus used in 1986. He and his dad were wrong.

looked like a Ping on steroids. Two more disparate putter types are hard to imagine, but the Response reflects the changes that Nicklaus's putting underwent as he neared the age of 50 and needed a more forgiving club. How like most golfers! For about a year after that putt, Mac-Gregor Responses sold like hotcakes. But then the demand disappeared. The oversized stick worked for Jack that week, but not for everyone.

The wacky story comes later, as Nicklaus has attempted to collect all the clubs he used to win his majors, and the Response was the only club still missing. He thought he'd found it once a few years ago. The story starts in 1988, when Nicklaus was at home getting ready for the Masters and future PGA Tour pro Chris Smith, a friend of Nicklaus's son Gary, was playing with him. Smith was snooping around in Jack's bag and saw a MacGregor Response. Nicklaus knew Smith was struggling with his putting and offered him the putter. "I told him there was no way I could take that putter," Smith recalls, but Nicklaus insisted. Fifteen years

THE BISHOP'S GREATEST ROUND
(AND WHAT HAROLD RAMIS WANTS YOU TO KNOW ABOUT GOD)

Something as complex and confusing as putting is bound to get wrapped up in something as complex and powerful as religion. The makers of The Way putter seem to feel that one illuminates the other, as they give a copy of the devotional book *In His*

Grip to everyone who buys the $189 stick (which has an H-shaped head for a high moment of inertia and can be adjusted in length and lie angle to be a belly putter or a standard stick, and even to be used sidesaddle). The putter's designer says on thewayputters.com, "I am confident that you will find 'the way' to better putting, but I am much more hopeful that you will find 'The Way' to eternal joy, peace and life. 'The Way' putter improves the golfer's ability to see the path of the putt and to follow through naturally to the cup."

The Way putter doesn't make any claims for getting you closer to God, and the Reverend Billy Graham himself once wittily suggested that if you can't putt, don't expect miracles. "Prayer never seems to work on the golf course. I think it has something to do with me being a terrible putter," he said.

But the movie *Caddyshack* goes the reverend one better. The putter as a being, putting as an expression of one's self, putting as a cosmic experience we're unable to explain—of course, the magisterial movie explores all of these notions—in the person of the Bishop, who rounds out the full assortment of human archetypes paraded through the movie. Here the Bishop finds himself having the round of his life in a thunderstorm of biblical force. Putt after putt veers into the hole as the Bishop sends his praises to the wet heavens. But on the 18th hole, he is forsaken and misses a crucial putt. "Rat farts!!" he bellows, and is struck by lightning. Putting, in almost all of its cosmic depth and silly absurdity, is summed up in this scene. A respected man of God willingly subsumes his entire being to the endeavor of putting and finds momentary rapture. Just as it appears he will achieve earthly perfection, he is struck down. Of all the possible ways, God has seized upon putting as a fitting demonstration of His many mysterious powers. Take solace in this if you've ever struggled on the green.

Later in the movie, Ted Knight's character is alarmed at the Bishop's drinking. "You're drinking too much, Your Excellency," he says. The Bishop responds, "Excellency, fiddlesticks! My name's Fred, and I'm just a man, same as you are." Knight responds, "You're not a man, you're a bishop, for God's sakes!" The Bishop shoots back, "There is no God." It seems putting has laid bare the Bishop's particular inner self: just a man with wavering faith. Pick up a putter at your own risk.

There's a cute footnote to the Bishop's

scenes, and it's that Henry Wilcoxon, who played
the Bishop, had played Pentaur in Cecil B. DeMille's
The Ten Commandments and the Vicar in the *Mrs.
Miniver* movies—an inspired inside joke by
producer Jon Peters and director Harold Ramis.

later, Smith had, by his own estimate, 2,500 clubs in his basement, and when he heard a Nicklaus associate mention that the Jack Nicklaus Museum in Columbus, Ohio, was lacking one crucial piece, he spoke up. But first he kidded the associate, "Ask Jack what he wants the putter for, because I'm putting it on eBay right now."

Smith went home and had his son, Cameron, pose with the putter, to commemorate the fact that the Smith residence had housed the famous stick for many years. He even had Cameron imitate the putter-in-the-air trot that forever identifies Nicklaus with that putt. Then he packed up the putter and sent it off—and Nicklaus discovered it wasn't the right one. It was a different Response, one that Nicklaus had owned in 1986 but hadn't used in the Masters. And there the story stands: the Jack Nicklaus Museum still lacks arguably the most famous one-putt putter ever.

CHAPTER 3

Sincerest Flattery: The Evolution of the Putter

Golf is a game whose aim is to hit a
very small ball into a very small hole,
with weapons singularly ill-designed
for that purpose.

— WINSTON CHURCHILL

Writers love to start with a quotation from a
famous person, and Winston Churchill is
one of our favorites. It gives us some credibility.

But this time Churchill's a bad idea, because he was wrong. Cute and clever, but wrong.

By Churchill's time, we humans had hit literally billions of golf shots, and our clubs were pretty doggone good. In fact, if our trial-and-error skills were so bad that Churchill's sticks, after centuries of golf evolution, were still "singularly ill-designed," then we humans never would have learned to make fire, never would have invented the wheel, and certainly never would have got around to golf clubs. In fact, Churchill's clubs were so evolved and so good that Tiger Woods could win with them today and you and I would probably play within a few strokes of our handicaps after getting used to them. Who knows, we might even play better, because we'd want to swing a little easier to help the heavier-shafted, less-forgiving clubs find the ball at the sweet spot.

So what the prime minister probably meant was that golf clubs hadn't yet succeeded in forgiving every flaw in our swings—in other words, that they were ill-suited to working miracles.

In Churchill's day, MacGregor made the beautiful Tommy Armour 693 woods and their close kin, the M85 Eye-O-Matic woods, which many top pros—Jack Nicklaus included—were still using in the 1980s. MacGregor's Tommy Armour irons—made for three decades starting in 1935—looked a lot like Tiger Woods's Nike blades today. Wilson's R-90 sand iron, endorsed by Gene Sarazen starting in 1933 and used for all manner of short shots by clever players, is almost a dead ringer for premium wedges now made by Cleveland, Titleist, Wilson, and dozens of other companies. Putters? You could buy a Bulls Eye putter then (though not yet produced by Acushnet), a Cash-In blade (made for 50 years

Winston Churchill golfing in 1913. He would later quip that golf clubs were "singularly ill-designed" for their purpose.

starting in the 1930s and used by many pros), or an Armour 3852S. The 3852S was modeled after the Spalding HB (introduced in 1919), and in turn inspired the famous Wilson 8802, which was introduced a few short years after Churchill left office for the second and last time.

So Churchill was passing the buck. But another thing that might have compelled him to dog the equipment of his generation is that every day for the past 120 years, frantic energy has been expended on designing a better club. (Before then, the energy was merely intense.) Proof is the tens of thousands of U.S. patents for golf clubs granted in the 20th century. Indeed, Churchill's excuse for calling his clubs "singularly ill-designed" might have been the club designers themselves, whose every "breakthrough" implies that previous models were second-rate.

Nowhere is the "breakthrough" mentality more apparent than with putters today. Callaway Golf calls its I-Trax putter "a revolution in accuracy." The stick has "interchangeable vision strips" that "give you the flexibility to choose the way you line up your putts, and send them straight into the heart of the cup." Apparently, the only barrier between golfers and the center of the cup these last 600 years has been the freedom to choose between straight-line and chevron markings on the top of the putter, a choice now made available by Callaway

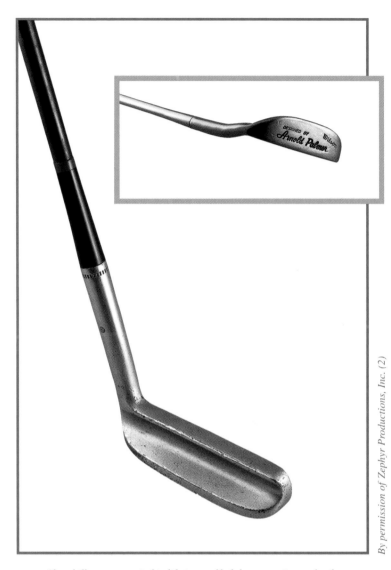

Churchill was wrong: in his lifetime, golf clubs were quite good—for example, the Armour 3852S and the Wilson Designed by Arnold Palmer, soon to be called The Wilson 8802.

Golf. "Discover a better game through better science," the I-Trax ad reads, recalling Churchill's contention that design has always been the problem, not the fact that it's just plain hard to have your putter on line and square to the hole when it makes contact with the ball—or that it's also hard to read greens, gauge speed, and swing accordingly.

The breathless claims putter companies make today highlight something else—one of the most important and charming facts about the history of the modern putter: there is almost literally nothing new under the sun. Nearly every important feature of the putter you use today was discovered, tried, and patented roughly 100 years ago. I could use this as an excuse to make fun of my putting and yours—"Dudes, we've had more than 100 years to get it right and we haven't, so we must just stink!"—but I won't. Instead, let's jump back and forth between today and a century ago to discover how long we golfers have been laboring over the same putter designs and how long putter designers have been struggling to come up with something better.

Face inserts. It's quite likely your putter has an insert in the face, not simply a smooth, sheer surface of the same metal the rest of the head is made of. For example, some of Srixon's putters use a lightweight aluminum alloy insert, which claims to offer superior sound and feel, for better distance control. Never Compromise's Gray Matter 2 putter has an "aluminum-infused weave" insert, which weighs less than traditional aluminum and allows more weight to be positioned outside and back of the sweet spot, for better putter control, says the company. Those are metal inserts, and Andy Brumer, in his clever book, *Guide to the Golf Revolution*, notes that you can also get putters with inserts of wolfram (a tungsten) or beryllium copper or "Cyanamet," Jack Nicklaus's proprietary metal, just in case any of this helps you sleep better.

But Odyssey started the current insert trend 10 years ago, with a polymer (plastic) insert it named Stronomic—a made-up term for a man-made material. You can still buy an Odyssey 2 with the Stronomic insert, and plenty of companies offer sticks with plasticky faces, but why stop at just plastic or just metal when you could buy Odyssey's White Steel with *both*—a milled lightweight steel insert surrounded by a Stronomic insert? The goal is the sound of a metal face with the touch of a polymer insert. But if this still isn't revolutionary enough for you, then try TaylorMade's Rossa putters with "AGSI" technology, in which a seven-metal alloy called "Titallium" forms the insert, which in turn is scored with 12 tiny grooves that are filled with a polymer. TaylorMade claims the cushy grooves impart a more immediate forward roll to the ball and keep it on line better. (It's not uncommon for putters to impart a little backspin or sidespin, due to their normal three- or four-degree loft).

As I write this, inserts are big, and they're expected to be big for a long time. But they're not new—not remotely. In the 1890s, W. Allaway of Edinburgh, Scotland, made a putter with an insert of gutta-percha, the hard-rubber, softer-than-metal substance that balls had been made with for nearly 50 years. Not only did the putter have an insert, the insert itself was scored—crudely, but in a way suggestive of TaylorMade's today—presumably to offer both feel and control at impact. Wood and leather inserts were tried in golf clubs a little later, and in 1915, Spalding came out with its Cork Center putter—a slender mallet with a cork face insert that was visible from the back as well.

So today's putter makers aren't on to anything radically new with inserts, no matter how breathless they get telling you about them. What they've done is improve, significantly, on an idea that was logical and good—but not at all new.

Let's look quickly at a few more such ideas. How

Courtesy of Srixon/SRI Sports

By permission of Zephyr Productions, Inc.

The Allaway Putter—a face insert long before they were cool; and Srixon's
P-410—the state of inserts 115 years later.

about the *mallet*? Today, Cobra Golf's King Cobra IM-02 offers a half-moon shape, a predominantly matte-silver head, and one alignment line running parallel to the face and two perpendicular at roughly a ball's width—quite like the Ray Cook M1-S, actually, which appeared more than four decades ago and won roughly 150 tournaments in the next dozen years. But the Ray Cook wasn't the first mallet putter, either. In fact, the *very first* putters were mallets, the circa-1750 Dickson putter being the oldest extant example. (The majority of clubs in Dickson's day were wooden mallets of various

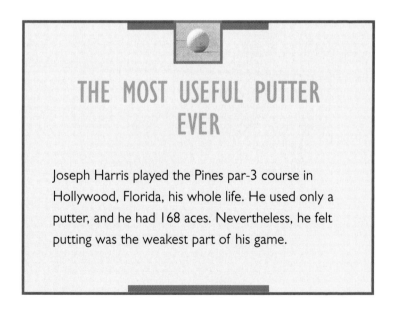

THE MOST USEFUL PUTTER EVER

Joseph Harris played the Pines par-3 course in Hollywood, Florida, his whole life. He used only a putter, and he had 168 aces. Nevertheless, he felt putting was the weakest part of his game.

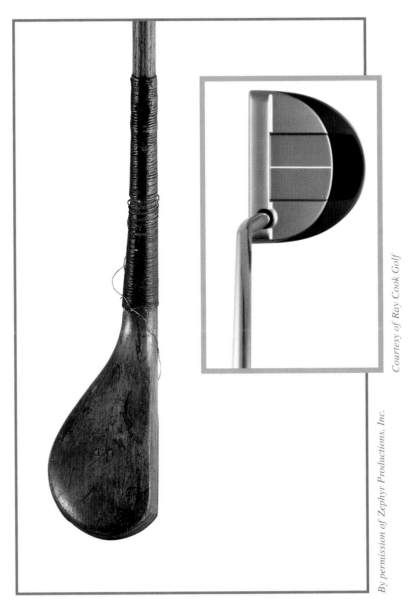

The Dickson and the Cobra IM-02: mallets 250 years apart.

sizes, used for everything from drives to putts—sometimes both drives *and* putts with the same club!)

Let's check out another improvement: *interchangeable head weights*. They're everywhere in today's clubs. TaylorMade's r7 driver has four interchangeable plugs and roughly a dozen "best" awards from authorities as varied as *Popular Science* and *Fortune* magazines. Louisville Golf's Stimp mallet putter has changeable weights in the face, and the Wilson Staff Kc4 has "weight ports" in the sole, for swing-weight adjustments corresponding to a golfer's preferences or a course's putting surfaces. These clubs represent the pinnacle of their makers' craft . . . more than 80 years after the Ellingham putter received a patent for removable weights held in place by a cap that threaded into the back of the head. And at least 10 years before that, the Strate-Put putter had a screw cap in its square toe, for access to a long chamber where a cylindrical weight could be added.

You're starting to get my point here, but let me putt out.

Center-shafted. Ben Hogan by Bettinardi's The Hawk BHB12 is one of the many current "game-improvement" putters with a shaft that meets just in back of the sweet spot, making the putter more forgiving of

The Ellingham of the 1920s and the Louisville Golf Stimp of today—
interchangeable head weights in both.

Bettinardi and Anderson: face-balanced putters a century apart.

off-center hits and easier to keep square at impact—much like the Anderson putter patented in Britain in 1892.

Spheres used as sight lines. You can't be a golfer and not know about today's Odyssey White Hot 2-Ball putter, the best-selling putter on earth since it was introduced early in 2002. Two white golf-ball-sized disks sit behind the sweet spot, leaving little to our haggard imaginations as we try to line up a putt. It looked very odd when it was introduced, but it actually derives from an idea of putting guru Dave Pelz, who fashioned a "3-ball" putter in the mid-1980s that the USGA outlawed, because it was deeper than its face was wide. Of course, the turn-of-the-20th century "Ball Back" iron had experimented with the same concept eight decades before—both as a sighting aid and a way of placing weight (probably too much weight!) behind the ball.

Let's stick with the Odyssey White Hot 2-Ball for a quick minute. A *flange*? *Face-balancing* and *heel-shafting* achieved via a *goose-neck*? A deep, narrowing head designed to spread weight low and back for stability (a quality also known as a *high moment of inertia*)? All of these are features of the Odyssey *and* of various turn-of-the-century putters!

So it's easy and fun to tweak club companies like

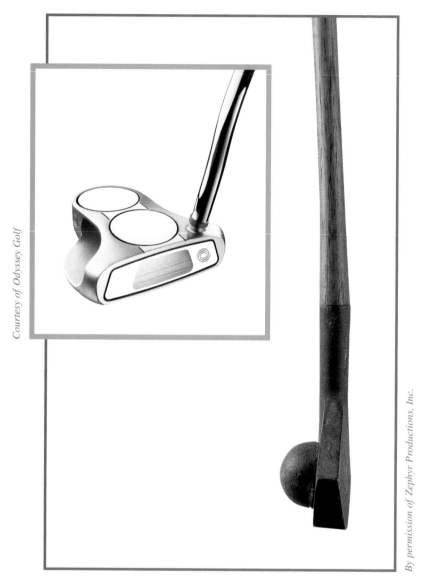

The Ball Back (right) *and the 2-Ball: the same idea, from slightly ridiculous to nearly sublime.*

Odyssey's parent, Callaway Golf, which grosses nearly $1 billion a year and accounts for nearly half of the money spent on putters in the United States annually. But that's not to say that current putters—Odyssey's or anyone else's—aren't better than those of a century ago. Actually, they're a lot better. They may not constitute "a revolution in accuracy," because the revolution was happening a century ago and, frankly, because the biggest problems in putting reside in our own hands, arms, shoulders, and eyes—oh, and in our brains—not in the club itself. But today's putters are profoundly refined and scientifically rock-solid. In fact, so are the other two key elements of putting—the ball and the green. And they play key roles in the evolution of the putter, just as it plays a key role in their evolutions.

So let's take a look at the fascinating evolution of the flat stick, starting with what we can surmise about the short game in the late Middle Ages, right on through the Ping Anser, the Acushnet Bulls Eye, and the Ram Zebra. What we'll see is that putters, balls, and greens have all undergone profound evolutions, especially in the last 150 years, and that they've brought out the best in one another. When we're done, you'll actually regard a putting green with a little less fear and loathing, for it's doing all it can to help you sink the putt.

As recently as 125 years ago, the putting green was a disaster. Before then, there really was no green as we know it; in fact, the whole course was called a green. A hole was cut in the ground, often with a knife, sometimes at a spot where the weather or grazing animals left the grass a little shorter, and golfers hit to the same hole for weeks or months, further battering the turf. To make matters worse, it was customary to tee off a few paces from the previous cup, which left divots and scuff marks precisely where today we expect carpetlike green or friendly fringe. You can thank the Royal and Ancient Golf Club of St. Andrews for a lot, including the invention of the dedicated tee area.

The lawn mower was also invented in England, in 1828, and its use became common at better courses there by the 1880s. Before they could invest in a mower, however, good courses employed men skilled in cutting grass with a scythe, and the best ones could trim a green to somewhere between an inch or two in height, according to Bob Labbance, coauthor of the fascinating book *Keepers of the Green: A History of Golf Course Management*. Even so, where we now have fringe, turn-of-the-20th-century accounts describe holes where foot-long unruly grass suddenly gives way to a tiny putting area. There are also descriptions, Labbance says, of square greens the size of small rooms. These late-19th-century greens were what we'd consider "chipping greens" today, Labbance told me. "We'd recognize them as greens, but you'd have to bash the ball."

Bash the ball. Does that sound like putting as we know it? Not at all, and keep that in mind as we consider, briefly, the golf ball that was used until the second half of the 19th century. For centuries, the common ball was a few leather strips sewn tightly together, then turned tanned-side-out, stuffed with "a top-hat full" of boiled and softened feathers, sewn closed, beaten into shape, and painted. It managed to turn out pretty hard—good players could send one more than 150 yards—but this ball could not be depended on to roll precisely where you aimed it, even if you were putting in the lobby of the Royal and Ancient. These balls were squirrelly enough that it took the "gutty"—the first rubber ball, made in 1845 out of gutta-percha—only 15 years to completely supplant the "featherie."

So until the mid-1800s, at least, greens were scruffy, pockmarked putting areas with no regularity in surface texture and often no demarcation from the rest of the course. "It was more like hitting toward a target, and there happened to be a hole there," Labbance says.

That explains the putters from the very beginnings

of golf until well into the 1800s: wooden-shafted and wooden-headed mallets shaped a bit like our hybrid woods but with elongated heads and often with long shafts, since they might do double duty as a short or long approach club. These clubs were expected to have less of the precision or "feel" of today's putters, and, apart from some extra weight low and behind the ball owing to their bulbous heads, they had none of the game-improvement features that I mentioned above as cropping up around the turn of the century. Those features simply wouldn't have been appreciated on hardscrabble, shaggy, or non-

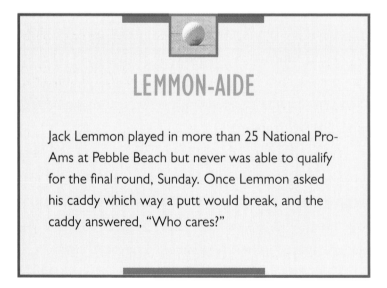

LEMMON-AIDE

Jack Lemmon played in more than 25 National Pro-Ams at Pebble Beach but never was able to qualify for the final round, Sunday. Once Lemmon asked his caddy which way a putt would break, and the caddy answered, "Who cares?"

existent greens, where play included rough-and-tumble tactics like the stymie, a feature of two-ball match play that lasted all the way to the middle of the 20th century. Before then, you didn't mark you ball if it was in your opponent's line; instead, he decided how to "negotiate" the stymie—whether to go around or through your ball using his putter, or *over* it, using an 8-iron or its earlier equivalent and possibly leaving a divot for the next group to contend with!

All of this goes a long way toward explaining why no one broke 80 on the Old Course at St. Andrews until 1858, two years before the first British Open. If the USGA really wanted to make the U.S. Open greens tough for the pros who love to complain about that tournament today, it could just re-create the greens conditions of 1850 and listen for the screams.

So as the 20th century drew nearer, the putting green was a friendlier place to be than it had ever been. The gutty ball—now made by machines—could be depended on to go where aimed, and mowers could trim grass to a uniform height of less than an inch. The science of turf management was growing, too—thanks in part to lucky accidents, like when famous greenskeeper (and eventual British Open winner) Tom Morris, while working at Prestwick around 1860, unwittingly discov-

FRIGHTFUL GREENS

In 1989, PGA Tour pros made 52 percent of their
putts from six feet and under. Today they make
nearly 54 percent—from *eight* feet and under.
Better putters, advancements in swing teaching,
and better practice habits (thanks to standards set
by the hardworking Tiger Woods and Vijay Singh)
are offered as causes. But if putting's better, why
haven't average scores on the PGA Tour gone
down during that stretch? It's that courses are
getting longer and greens are getting smaller, so
between the tee and eight feet from the pin, it's
harder than ever. "Look what they've done to
Augusta lately, making the greens so tiny," says
M. G. Orender, honorary president of the PGA of
America and a golf pro and course developer
himself. "That was not what Bobby Jones
intended."

ered topdressing. He spilled a wheelbarrow of sand on an ailing green, spread the sand around rather than picking it up grain by grain, and in a few days discovered that the green had come back to life!

In this kinder environment, it paid to try to refine the putter, because you no longer needed to bash the ball, and if you were going to capitalize, you needed a club that responded to your efforts to make the ball do your bidding. Between 1890 and 1920—and in step with huge advances in manufacturing and materials technology in the world at large, by the way—the putter underwent enormous changes, arguably greater than at any time since. These changes had to contribute to a serious attack on record scores. The British Open 72-hole record dropped 10 strokes between 1899 and 1909. Contrast that with modern scoring records: it took 20 years for the Masters scoring record to drop 10 strokes after its inception in 1934, and since Ben Hogan shot a 274 in 1953, the record has dropped only 4 strokes.

Putters weren't the only part of golf being revolutionized around the turn of the 20th century—for instance, the wound ball was invented in 1899 and held sway as the choice of pros for 90 years—but putters spurred the most intense invention.

The flange, the center-shaft, the center-shaft with

gooseneck, the face insert, the offset hosel, the removable weight, back-weighting, hollow areas in the head, the extended sight line—all of these legitimate advances emerged roughly between 1890 and 1910 and were part of the most important putters of the 20th century, including those we use today. Let's chronicle this history by looking at a few of the most famous putters of the modern era, starting with the Schenectady, which is where any modern history has to start.

Right after the turn of the 20th century, a General Electric engineer in Schenectady, New York, invented a putter that combined a center shaft set slightly back from a low-profile face, and a sleek mallet shape that set a fair amount of weight low and back from the ball and was pleasing to the eye. If you walked onto the practice green with one today, you'd get some bemused looks, because we tend to prefer tomorrow's technology to yesterday's. But no one would be shocked if you started draining putts with it, because intuitively it looks like a good putter. In fact, apart from some cosmetic tweaks that aid alignment, it's astonishingly like the Advance Putter that was hailed on the cover of *Golf Illustrated* almost 70 years later, in 1971.

Top golfers started winning with the Schenectady almost immediately after it was introduced, and when

The Schenectady, the first breakthrough putter.

By permission of Zephyr Productions, Inc.

American finesse player Walter Travis won the British Amateur Championship in 1904 over long-hitting British opponents, the R&A (the rules-making body in Britain) took note, finally making all center-shafted putters illegal in 1910—the most significant rules difference with the USGA in history. The British ban on this frighteningly good and untraditional feature lasted 41 years.

Meanwhile, in the United States, several *center-*

shafted blades were starting to attract widespread attention, and they'd go on to amass hundreds of tournament wins. These putters had simple, slender, squarish heads and—significantly—shafts that met the head roughly midway between the heel and the sweet spot, a compromise that allowed for some of the feel of a heel-shafted putter and some of the pendulum-inducing balance of a full-on center-shafted putter. Spalding's Cash-In putter was made for five decades starting in the 1930s, and was the favorite of countless pros. (And if you started playing golf anytime during this period, your first set probably had a knockoff of the Cash-In for you to learn with.) Roughly a decade after the Cash-In came the Bulls Eye putter, sort of a swishier version of the Cash-In, with a stylish, rounded heel spur and a beautifully colored soft brass head. You might have bought a Bulls Eye—made by Acushnet starting in 1968—as your first serious putter after you outgrew the Cash-In copy. Or you might have bought a Walter Hagen Tom Boy, which combined some of the Bulls Eye's curves and its no-hosel design with the Cash-In's slightly squarer dimensions. If so, you'd have been in good company: Kathy Whitworth earned all of her 88 tournament wins with a Tom Boy. Cash-In, Bulls Eye, Tom Boy—these slender putters were exemplars of simplicity and balance, and they tell us that putting greens

The Bulls Eye, the Tom Boy, and the Cash-In: graceful mid-20th century blades that knew how to make putts.

were a helluva lot better in the middle of the 20th century than they had been 50 or 100 years before. These putters were made for stroking and finessing, not for bashing!

Where the Schenectady and its many bulbous offspring looked solidly reassuring to a player's eye, and where center-shafted blades looked sleek and sophisticated, the extensive and long-lived family of *flanged blades* has always looked just right. There's relatively little difference between the Spalding HB putter introduced in 1919 and the Tommy Armour 3852S putter produced between 1935 and 1967. Or between those and the Wilson Designed by Arnold Palmer putter (introduced in 1962, soon renamed The 8802, and produced for more than 30 years) or the George Low 600 (also introduced in 1962 and marketed under the Bristol and Sportsman brands). And they're all clearly predecessors of the Odyssey PM Prototype blade used by Phil Mickelson today. But it takes a serious touch—like Mickelson's—to putt masterfully with this kind of putter. Its game-improvement features are few—a slight flange at the rear and sometimes an offset to give a clear view of a simple, thin topline. Its soft metal and minimalist lines are for the natural, "touch" player, and its shaft joins the head right at the heel, for a player who has a "screen-door" swing (open on backswing, returning to

The George Low blade accompanied Jack Nicklaus on 15 major victories.
Today, Phil Mickelson (above) *often uses that putter's handsome*
offspring, an Odyssey prototype blade.

square at impact) and the touch to make it happen again and again. It's true that many more players used this kind of putter 30 and 40 years ago than today; Nicklaus himself won 15 of his 20 majors with a George Low, and Ben Crenshaw won all but two of his tournaments with an 8802. But it's a measure of how much putters have evolved since then that only the players with supreme touch find this putter the most effective today.

The rest of us need a little help finding the sweet spot, and that's why Karsten Solheim is our patron saint. Solheim was an engineer for General Electric (sound familiar?) in the early 1960s, with a steady but unspectacular custom-order putter business, called Ping, on the side. He had designed and produced 21 different putter models when he set himself to unseating the classic Wilson Arnold Palmer putter, which, it seemed to him, all the pros were playing with at the time. His designs had already thrown classic lines out the window; Solheim was a game-improvement man from the time he eight-putted his first golf hole, at the age of 42. His putters were mechanical and robotic looking, and none was more so than the Anser, his 1966 "answer" to the Palmer putter challenge, which he first sketched on the dust jacket of a record album, probably because the hole in the jacket was roughly the size of a cup.

The Anser was heel-shafted (for a good view of the clubface) but face-balanced (for stability) thanks to a radical gooseneck that recalled some turn-of-the-20th century right-turns. It's been called "the plumber's neck" informally ever since. It had a hollow area behind the ball, and most of its weight was concentrated at the edges for a wider and more forgiving sweet spot, like a tennis racket, in Solheim's reasoning mind. It had a long, terraced flange, for additional moment-of-inertia support. It's now one of the two or three best-selling putters of all time, and here's proof of how rock-solid Solheim's design was: 40 years after the Schenectady putter was invented, no one was making that precise putter anymore, although its design principles were still being used; 40 years after the Anser debuted, Ping still makes the Anser—and dozens of other companies make essentially the same putter. If the Anser itself isn't the best-selling putter of all time, the Anser style is.

And it's not just for players whose games need improving. Tiger Woods uses Scotty Cameron's version of the Anser, the Newport, and not because he doesn't have fantastic touch; but because the Anser's face-balancing rewards players who have a consistent pendulum-style stroke like Woods's, with less of the open-and-close motion that blade users tend to have.

Not in question: the Ping Anser is the best-selling putter design ever.

In looking at some of the seminal putters of the 20th century, we've identified two strains—the refined blade putters used by most golfers until the Anser came along, and the game-improvement putters, which have had a steady presence since the turn of the 20th century but have become the focus of putter makers in the past 40 years. The blades had the power of tradition, and since they were what most good golfers grew up with, you often found them in the hands of great players like Nicklaus, Palmer, and Crenshaw. The game-improvement sticks, by contrast, tended to make a big splash, as when the Schenectady provoked a major rule implementation in 1910—or when the Zebra putter came out in 1975.

If you never putted with a Zebra, ask your dad about it. The simple, shapely mallet had 11 black stripes covering its head, leaving nothing to the imagination where alignment is concerned. This reflected inventor Dave Taylor's belief that misalignment becomes more common as a golfer gets older, that it gets harder and harder to translate the putter face's topline (running north-south) into the correct line for your putt (running east-west). Remember, until this time you got, at most, two small aimlines at the top of a putter, and many putters came with none. Jack Nicklaus had to cut the aimlines into his favorite George Low blade with a hacksaw, and the reason he had two was that he botched the first one and located it off center, so he had to cut a matching one to frame the sweet spot! So the Zebra's long, thick stripes looked radical—the putter couldn't have been introduced before the hip 1970s—but it proved the adage that what works on the green quickly looks good. Taylor's friend Gene Littler demolished the competition with an early Zebra at the 1975 Bing Crosby National Pro-Am in swirling winds at Pebble Beach, and he rode the club to his most lucrative year as a pro. The Zebra hit the commercial market a few months later, in May. You can still get a current version of the Zebra, but while the putter is universally respected among putter mavens, it's lost its cachet.

After all, if you want a putter with a nice big face, lots of weight stretching back behind the ball, and sighting aids that scream "Here's your line!" there's the Odyssey White Hot 2-Ball. This curious-looking club was introduced to pro golfers around the world in late October 2001, and that week, 23 of them switched to it. One, Paul Lawrie, sank a 65-foot birdie putt on the 18th hole of the Old Course at St. Andrews to win the Dunhill Links Championship. Three years later, the putter accounted for $142 million of Callaway Golf's revenues—and roughly one-third of all putter sales in the United States. It doesn't command that market share today, but

The Zebra: opening golfers' eyes to better alignment.

only because every self-respecting big putter company has a 2-Ball-like putter in its lineup—although none has a putter with two circles to help you aim. Callaway has gone to court to see to that.

Proponents say the White Hot 2-Ball balances like a smaller club, forgives mishits as well as any putter, and is a (relative) breeze to align, thanks to the literal-as-can-be golf-ball-sized circles on its head. The circle idea is so reassuring, Odyssey is coming out with a 3-Ball putter (you knew it had to happen) as I write this book.

The Zebra was a splendid putter, but there's a feeling that putter technology lagged behind other clubs in the years between the Anser and the 2-Ball. Who can argue with the impact of metal woods, after all? But the 2-Ball highlights the fact that the past five or six years have been the most creative for putters since the 1960s—and maybe since the turn of the 20th century.

Why all this technology? And why now? Technology generally doesn't evolve faster than the problems it has to solve, so many of the high-tech refinements in today's putters would have been like pearls before swine on the shaggy greens of 50 and 100 years ago. Longtime USGA rules chief Frank Thomas estimates the greens Bobby Jones putted on would have registered no more than a 5 on today's Stimpmeter, a third as fast as the fastest U.S. Open greens today. And Labbance says that Sherwood Moore, Winged Foot's famous superintendent, told him that course's greens probably would have Stimped at a 7 at the 1959 U.S. Open, as they were cut to about one-quarter inch in length. For a frame of reference, today's bad municipal course would Stimp an 8, Labbance says. Casual golfers tend to like shaggy greens, but pros want them glassy, up to a point, since pros tend to trust their greens-reading skills and like a green that does what it should do. (Everybody fears contours, of course.) But regardless of your skill level, on faster greens, you need more "feel." Putters of today are intensely refined—are so good at giving us that feel, plus helping us aim and forgiving us when our swing doesn't obey—because today's greens are like pool tables compared to those of 50 and 100 years ago. And at major pro events, they virtually *are* pool tables, Stimping at 13 or higher after being cut in two to four directions each morning at a height of 9/100th of an inch, nearly twice as short as just 10 years ago. In 1997, Paul Stankowski prepped for the Masters by putting on his garage floor for 15 minutes a day. He three-putted only twice at Augusta and tied for fifth. So if you want to understand the history of the putter, recall what Byron Nelson said when he was asked what has been the most important technological innovation in golf: "The lawn mower."

CHAPTER 4

The Pros: Inconsistent for the Sake of Consistency

L et's talk about them and us.

The big difference between the pros and us isn't their distance, because a lot of amateurs can hit a golf ball as far as many pros. And it's not their shotmaking ability, or creativity, because most golf shots really aren't that fancy. Aim and shoot. Course management? Pros know more about this than we do, because it's their job. But that doesn't mean they're all great at it. It took Phil Mickelson 10 years of also-ran status at majors before he stopped trying to crush the course and started managing it—and won the Masters.

No, the big difference between them and us—besides the fact that they get to drive free cars every week—is their consistency. We love golf because there's always a chance we'll hit a shot exactly the way Tiger hits it. Tiger is Tiger because he almost *always* hits the shot the way Tiger hits it. These guys (and the women, too) can do it over and over and over again, even under pressure. Tiger Woods has hit plenty of breathtaking shots.

But he's just as mesmerizing on the practice green in his consistency. Check him out next time you're at a PGA Tour event. He'll be in the very middle of the green with his coach, and nobody will interrupt them. At some point Tiger will practice four-footers with the aid of a little chute that forces him to keep the putter head square and on line. Fans will congregate four deep to watch him, and before one Buick Open we watched him drain at least four dozen of these short ones in a row. It may have been more than four dozen, but I lost my concentration and lost count. Meanwhile, Tiger just kept his head down and kept putting. See what I mean about them versus us?

Now, do you want to know a true similarity between them and us? They're almost never satisfied with their putters either. You'll be astonished to learn that almost one-quarter of the field at every PGA Tour event is using

SCOTSMAN TRIES TO PURCHASE TALENT

Golf enthusiast Neil McLellan, a Scotsman, died in 2005 and left behind 3,000 clubs that he'd purchased through the years in a vain effort to get his handicap to stop hovering around 18. The sticks were discovered in a large shed behind his house and sold for £30,000 ($60,000), roughly 60 percent of what he paid for them. Most of the clubs had been used only once. "He was always aware of his eccentricity but was unable to do anything to combat it," his lawyer said. "He would try one set of clubs, get frustrated, toss them aside and buy another set." His "collection," the largest private one known, included 185 putters.

a different putter than the previous week. At the Masters—where the greens are Stimpmeter-13 tough on Sunday—more like 30 percent of the golfers are trusting a new putter.

It's kind of nice to know that the pros are aren't consistent in everything.

There are three kinds of pros where putters are concerned, according to Robert Evans, director of tour operations for MacGregor Golf. That title means Evans stands beside that practice green, next to a bagful of MacGregor Bobby Grace putters, and does whatever a pro wants done to his putter, whether he's under contract to MacGregor or not. It's all about getting Bobby Grace putters in as many pros' bags as possible, in case one wins the tournament—which has been proven to make golfers worldwide ask, "What was in his bag?"

So Evans knows whereof he speaks when he says, "There's the fickle guy. He changes putters every week. There's the finicky guy. He notices any change in loft, lie, vibration, noise—some of these guys have the greatest hearing in the world for things nobody else hears. But he does—or he feels it. And he makes us change it. There's a third one: stubborn. Stubborn would be a guy who stays with a particular putter always, when he's putting terribly. He won't look for help. He'll just stay in that rut."

Doesn't it sound like a bunch of kooks in FootJoys?

We'll talk more about all of these types, and we'll add one more: the lucky ones who don't change putters

GO FIGURE

Golf-club companies' tour reps are smart enough not to make sociological or genetic generalizations, but more than one of them will tell you that LPGA pros are more likely to make a last-minute change in putters than PGA Tour pros are. "I've seen women not happy on Wednesday and take something completely new on the course on Thursday," said Mike Eggeling, the tour rep for Never Compromise. "I don't want to get into the gender-based things and blame it on that. It's just what I've seen."

Whatever the reason, some of the best "last-minute-decision" stories involve women. Jerry Walters, Yes! Golf's tour rep, tells of how Courtney Wood, a golf-store salesperson from Tennessee, showed up at his studio the morning of the U.S. Women's Open and wanted Yes! Golf's computerized stroke analysis and a new putter. "I'm thinking, this is maybe the most important tournament she'll ever play, why not use what brought her?" But Wood had detected a flaw. "We showed her the difference on camera of the ball-roll she was getting from a very popular brand that rhymes with 'Schmodyssey' and has two white disks on the back—I don't want to name names—and one of ours," Walters says. Armed with a Yes!, Wood finished almost last in the Open. Oh, well.

Now, Moira Dunn had better luck with a last-minute switch. She won her first LPGA event after 245 starts in 2004—with a putter she'd bought the night before the tournament. She and some friends went to a golf store to buy glow-in-the-dark balls; Dunn came away with a $190 Bettinardi Big Ben in addition. She balked hard at the price—then won $150,000 that week in her first win in a decade as a pro.

At the other end of the fame spectrum from Dunn and Wood is Michelle Wie. One club rep said he made her eight different putters in the two days before a tournament—and she didn't play with a single one of them that week. Again, oh, well.

There are explanations for the ladies' changeability that don't involve the extra X chromosome—such as, women pros are less likely to have a putter contract that limits the number of events in which they can use a competitor's model. "Look at the [logos on] golf bags out here. It's more Kraft/Nabisco than club companies," Walters says. (Often, putter contracts call for 20 appearances each season with a company's flat sticks, allowing a handful of opportunities to experiment.)

And you know what? The men on the Nationwide Tour—most of them without putter deals—are also capricious. "At one Nationwide event we'd had two putters in play the week before and we ended up with 12 this time," says Robert Evans, MacGregor's tour rep. "That would never happen on the PGA Tour."

because they don't need to and don't want to. Woods has won nine majors with the same putter, a German stainless steel Scotty Cameron Ping Anser–style stick. He's used just three putters since college. Ben Crenshaw used the same putter—"Little Ben," a Wilson 8802 blade—for more than a quarter century, starting when he was 16. Gary Player used the same putter for 27 straight seasons.

Ernie Els has used only a handful of putters during his career. "Ernie was the lowest-maintenance player I've had," says Byron Eder, who oversees the Rossa line of putters for TaylorMade as its pro-tour technician. "We had him for two years, and I'd always make him something new and tell him I had it, but he never switched and never asked for anything new. He won the British in 2002 with one of my putters, and the only things he asked me to do all year were change the grip before he won at Doral and the loft before he won the British."

Most players would love to be like Els, but they're not. Evans says he once watched Chad Campbell on the practice green until 6:30 p.m. the Wednesday before the Tour Championship (that's late—you're supposed to be having a beer by then) practicing four-footers and making one-quarter of them. Campbell was a Titleist user then, but Evans believes Campbell was sticking with the putter not because of an endorsement deal but because he felt that "if he's not putting well, it must be something he's doing." In 2005 Campbell switched from his Titleist blade to a Guerin Rife mallet—and saw immediate improvement. He was roughly 70th on the tour in putting in 2005, after being a lousy 160th in 2004. Says Evans, "At the Players, I was watching him and thinking, 'If he could putt, he'd win so much money, because he hits the balls so well.' "

So who's the anti–Chad Campbell? Maybe Bob Estes. "He's one of our players. He uses a different putter every week," says Never Compromise tour rep Mike Eggeling. Or Neal Lancaster? "It's kind of a joke. He changes every week—which is fine, because he's easy to work with," says Larry Watson, tour rep for Titleist's Scotty Cameron putters and brother of a guy named Tom. Estes and Lancaster would be the fickle ones. Mark Calcavecchia? "There's a guy who has the biggest problem in the world getting comfortable with a putter sometimes," Watson says. Rich Beem? "He's always looking at the loft, the lie, the grip—how's it feel today?" says Jon Laws, Callaway's tour rep. "Honestly," Beem himself told the *Chicago Tribune,* "I could change putters every week. I just like shaking things up."

Calcavecchia and Beem would be the finicky ones. Jesper Parnevik's in this camp, too. He's practiced with hundreds of putters in his career, and he spends up to eight hours a week before tournaments fussing with new ones. It's said he can travel with five putters from five different companies. But he's fussy about everything. He demanded lime-green and purple shoes in shades that took FootJoy 12 weeks to produce. In fact, he might be fussiest about his clothes. He obsessed so much over packing the right clothes for the 2005 Mas-

See the putter? There's a good chance Rich Beem had used a different one the week before—and yet another the week after.

ters that he forgot his clubs at home in West Palm Beach. Tiger Woods had to bring them to Augusta for him. "Of all the people to do that," Tiger said later. "He thinks the clothes in his closet are more important than his clubs."

The fickle/finicky bit can get more absurd. At the Bay Hill Invitational in 2002, Charles Howell III used three different putters (and two different grips) in four rounds on the way to finishing tied for 69th out of the 74 who made the cut. Eder said he once made a player eight putters in three days before the Players Championship—and the guy used none of them. Arnold Palmer may have used 2,000 different putters over a half century, according to some estimates. Still need evidence?

No, and it's refreshing to discover how desperate our heroes are for a putter with a new look and a better feel. "Sometimes you just get used to something and seeing it all the time. . . . You just can't distinguish where you're aiming. Sometimes it's just good to make a change," Cristie Kerr told *Golf World*.

It should be pointed out that pro golfers aren't this way with their irons. They'll ask for loft and lie adjustments, but you don't usually see players with a whole new bag of forged blades, because it takes time to learn exactly how far you hit a particular iron with a particular swing, and if there's one thing that can unglue a pro, it's when his or her feel for distance disappears on approach shots.

But the fact is, when pros switch putters, it often

works. Vijay Singh broke out a new one at the 2004 Buick Open—and won six of his next eight events on the way to $11 million in earnings that year. And this was no small tweak: he went from a pendulum-swinging belly putter to a heel-toe-weighted traditional stick.

In 2005, he switched from the heel-toe model to a mallet at the Buick Open, and putted lights-out on the way to a victory. Hank Kuehne tried out a Bobby Grace MOI (one of the newer space-age-looking mallets) right before the BellSouth Classic in 2003. Lo and behold, it ended up in his bag and the often-inconsistent Kuehne finished tied for third, then followed up tied for second at Houston the next week—a $544,000 haul, with some of the best putting of his season. And there's the example of Els noted earlier—two tweaks all season, both contributing to victories.

Good examples, but there are a million more. The hard-core golf magazines chronicle the phenomenon each week, with reports that read, "[Player X] switched to a [Putter Y] at [Tournament Z] and finished [decent ranking] in putts per greens in regulation, better than his season rank of [lousy]."

So what's going on here? Why do pro golfers change putters so often? Golf psychologists say the new stick sharpens up all the senses and mechanisms that create the putt. The new putter's head and topline recalibrate

Look closely at the Bettinardi in Vijay Singh's hands: after switching to it in 2004, he won six of his next eight tournaments.

Andy Lyons/Getty Images

a player's aim. The new grip heightens the sense of contact with the club and hence of control. A half inch more shaft or a degree change in lie angle can relax or support the body, sort of like rolling over in bed. Then there's the new sound. Sound truly is a key component of "feel," despite the apparent misnomer. Most good golfers prefer a specific type of sound, and to them it can connote hardness and precision or softness and "touch"—even though, for marketing purposes, some (relatively) soft putters can be made to sound hard and vice versa, depending on the types of metals, inserts, face widths, and other features of materials and geometry. And all golfers "feel" with their ears. "Put [soundproof] headphones on a player and ask him which putter feels best. They can't do it," said Taylor Made putter engineer Jose Miraflor a few years ago. "Eighty percent of what we feel is what we hear." (Billy Casper said his superb putting touch was developed in after-dark putting contests with his childhood buddies, when his other senses were attuned to the ball.) Thus, a pleasing new sound can sharpen the ears and stoke the confidence—especially in a pro. Brad Faxon, whose 1.704 putts per green in regulation in 2000 was the lowest ever, astonished a visiting journalist once when he took out four distinct types of Titleist balls, bounced each one on the face of his Scotty Cameron, and insisted they all sounded different to him. So sound matters—along with all the other putter characteristics that play into a pro's stroke and confidence.

Trouble is, they can matter too much. In duffers and pros alike, there's a point at which the problem simply isn't the stick but the golfer—his mechanics, his head, or both. But those are harder to work on than putter shopping—or putter hunting. There's a famous story about Lee Trevino rummaging around in a used-club barrel and finding the putter he used to win the British Open in 1972. The press reported this, and it sent golfers everywhere on a holy-grail search for the perfect used putter. Think about it: golf might be the most precise, scientific, rational, mechanical, geometrical game on earth, and despite this—or maybe because of this—golfers want to solve their problems through luck, magic, or happenstance. Irrational means, all of them.

This irritates Dave Pelz, the NASA scientist turned putting guru, whose 400-page *Putting Bible* aims to debunk about 400 golf canards. He writes, "For every [Trevino] story I've heard over the years, I know of maybe a thousand cases of my students picking up new putters that ruined (or at least damaged) their putting." Pelz the scientist notes that Trevino's putter wasn't magic—it just put his hands in a better position, "helping him putt better because it helped his already smooth-as-silk stroke." Pelz believes that while a poorly fit putter can hurt your game, a perfectly fit putter usually will only *not hurt* you. Pelz finds the answer to putting problems in objective factors—stance and grip, green-reading and pre-putt routine, tempo and distance—not in the inexplicable magic of a newfound putter. So he also tells his students to get fit for the proper putter, then stick with it for at least six months. That's how long he feels it takes his own rational teachings to take deep root in a golfer.

The way Pelz urges consistency and predictability only highlights how swashbuckling many pros are on the green. You see it when they not only switch putters but switch to a putter that requires a completely different stroke. There are dozens of putting strokes, if you want to start analyzing the minute movements of shoulders, arms, wrists, and hands, and the various stances that form the foundation. But broadly speaking, every stroke involves some rotation of the putter head around the shaft—just like every other golf shot. But the rotation can be almost negligible (a true pendulum stroke), or pretty dramatic (as in the strokes Ben Crenshaw and Phil Mickelson employ when using their traditional blades). Pelz would love it if most casual golfers eliminated that screen-door effect, but most pros already have a preferred stroke, and they use a putter that complements it—a more heel-shafted style (like Mickelson's blades) for the screen-door types and a more center-shafted model (like Tiger's Scotty Cameron Newport) for the pendulum type.

Until their quest for some magic compels them to switch putters *and* strokes. Jack Nicklaus, according to observers, changed strokes not only from event to event but from hole to hole. He would bring several putters with him to a tournament—it was all about what gave him touch and feel. In 2003, Mickelson shifted from his heel-shafted Scotty Cameron JAT to a center-shafted Cameron Futura because he had been pulling putts, overrotating the clubhead. "I want the characteristics of my putter to suit my style at a given moment," he said. Nicklaus and Mickelson have been great putters, and another current pro, Dudley Hart, has had some terrific years, too. He will switch between a Scotty Cameron Newport 2 (Cameron's take on the classic center-shafted Ping Anser) and a Cameron Bulls Eye. "He knows what both's characteristics are, and when he wants to go to a different stroke, he knows what he's getting into," said Cameron rep Watson. "Some of these guys out here have four or five different strokes."

In great feel putters like Nicklaus and Mickelson, switching strokes and getting away with it are a sign of genius and creativity, similar to the way former baseball pitching greats Luis Tiant and David Cone would switch grips and windups on the fly to suit a particular situation. It's how they *keep* their consistency, not *find* it. In lesser pros, switching is a sign of struggle. In the rest of us, it's Pelz's worst nightmare—the renunciation of reason. But isn't that the definition of putting?

CHAPTER 5

What's In a Name?
Well, Not Arrogance

Putting is a lot like NASCAR. You never know when you're going to end up with your wheels in the air or flames coming out of your tailpipe, metaphorically speaking. Mindful of the risks in their business, NASCAR drivers rarely give their cars grandiose nicknames. There's been Underbird and Heads Up! There's been Lars and even Shania. It's exactly the same way on the high-speed greens of the PGA Tour. Pro golfers never name their putter Killer.

Actually, it's uncommon for a pro golfer to name a putter at all. Give something a name and it says you expect to keep it around for a long time, like a child or a pet. It suggests friendship, trust, and permanence, and those usually aren't part of the putter relationship. In fact, wacky 1930s pro Ky Laffoon called all of his putters the same thing: My Little Sonofabitch. Where we do find a pro on a first-name basis with a putter, the name rarely makes big claims. There are no "Killers" or "One-Putts." Instead, there's often a reverent, cautious, or even ironic attitude in the names.

Scotswoman Dorothy Campbell was a very fine amateur golfer on both sides of the Atlantic for almost 50 years. She won the U.S. Women's Amateur at the age of 26, then again at 41 after completely reworking her unorthodox swing and adopting the Vardon grip that became prevalent while she was in semiretirement. She was a great chipper and putter who once finished Augusta National in 19 putts. She named her favorite putter Stella (and her favorite gooseneck mashie chipping club Thomas). The personal associations are unclear, but regardless, could a name sound less threatening?

After Mark Calcavecchia won the Subaru Sarazen World Open in 1997, he nicknamed the putter he'd used "Gene," after Sarazen himself—a reverent, maybe even superstitious, thank-you to the old man. "And the putter I won everything with in the late '80s," Calcavecchia said a few years ago, "is 'Billy,'" after the putter Ted Knight pleaded with in *Caddyshack*. ("Billy, Billy, Billy, Billy, Billy, Billy. Ooooh, Billy, Billy Billy" might be the ten most pathetic words ever uttered on the silver screen.) Added Calcavecchia: "I still visit those guys once in a while and look at 'em and say, 'Man, I used to make everything with you.'"

"Old Faithful" is what Arnold Palmer called the Wilson 8802 flanged-blade putter he used for some of his career. The name has an affectionate feel, and although it's not exactly arrogant, it *is* unreasonable. A great, charging, confident putter when he was young, Arnold struggled during the last 15 years of his career and took to carrying dozens of putters to each tournament, unsure of which would feel best. Old Faithful may have gotten old, but it wasn't faithful.

Ben Crenshaw got "Little Ben" when he was 16 years old, and Little Ben was with him for all but two of his pro victories. He first saw the Wilson 8802 on the rack at his home course, next to a handful of other 8802s that were just a bit heavier and a bit darker and not quite right. Ben was just back from the U.S. Amateur, and his dad surprised him by buying the stick without hesitation. His dad also named it, having in mind the proper names Bobby Jones gave his clubs, like Jeannie Deans (after Sir Walter Scott's strong and moral 18th-century heroine)

This putter had no name until Mark Calcavecchia won the Subaru Sarazen World Open in 1997. Then it became "Gene."

and Calamity Jane, the 19th-century cowgirl whose fictional alter ego probably had more adventures than she did.

Would you believe that Crenshaw wasn't using Little Ben in his first Masters win, in 1984? He was using a Cleveland Classics putter that belonged to his then-and-current manager Scott Sayers, because his bag had been stolen out of his car, right out of his own driveway, and wasn't found for three weeks. Crenshaw's wife, Julie, nicknamed the replacement putter "Little Scotty" (naturally).

But Little Ben and Little Scotty weren't names like Jeannie Deans and Calamity Jane. "Little" is sweet and affectionate—and docile, not like Bobby Jones's names.

The great Jones was the rare pro who allowed big claims to be made for his putter. "Calamity Jane" already was named when a club pro gave it to Jones right before the 1923 U.S. Open, which he won. When the putter wore out, he had another made and kept the name. With his open stance and wristy, slappy stroke, Jones was one of golf's greatest putters. He was also a ruthless perfectionist. Apparently, he felt no pressure from the claims made by Calamity Jane.

Nor did Jack Nicklaus in the case of "White Fang." He borrowed an Acushnet Bulls Eye from a friend of

Ben Crenshaw made his name with "Little Ben,"
the beloved putter he bought in high school. But
he won his first Masters with a stand-in, "Little
Scotty," shown here, after his bag was stolen. Little
Ben is in Crenshaw's bag still, and Little Scotty is
back with Crenshaw's agent, Scott Sayers.

(then-player, later PGA commissioner) Deane Beman in 1967 right before the U.S. Open. Nicklaus had been in a putting funk, carrying a dozen putters with him to each tournament. But he broke the Open scoring record with the putter that week and added four more PGA Tour wins with it before moving on to a new stick. Before Nicklaus got it, the putter's face had been painted white to reduce glare (you'd be surprised how happily pros deface their putters, even today, to make them look more agreeable or aim better). In Nicklaus's possession, it became known as White Fang, after the half-dog, half-wolf protagonist who grows up the hard way in Jack London's novel.

Nicklaus has said that he believes he's going to make every putt as he strokes it—and he doesn't putt until he believes it. It takes that kind of confidence to live with a putter called White Fang. Today, you don't find putter companies giving their sticks names so straightforwardly assured. Bettinardi Golf has the Baby Ben, which was conceived as Baby B, then informally called Baby Ben, since it was a version the Big Ben putter Bettinardi was marketing under the Ben Hogan umbrella at the time. But the Hogan company didn't like the name "Baby Ben," according to Bob Bettinardi, the company's founder. Before they all could settle on a new name, Jim Furyk won the 2003 U.S. Open with a prototype and raved on ESPN about the Baby Ben, after which the company had no choice but to keep the name. "Hundreds of thousands of people had heard it," Bettinardi explains.

Now, Yes! Golf, the boutique putter maker whose sticks have the dashing yellow and black grips, didn't back into the idea of naming their putters after people. They name them after women "because we like women a lot better than we like men," says Jerry Walters, Yes!'s tour technician. Recently, Retief Goosen has had an endorsement deal with TaylorMade for putters, but he can use other companies' sometimes, and he won the U.S. Open in 2001 with a Yes! prototype. So the company named the model after Goosen's wife, Tracy. "We were thinking, 'We can't pay him, but we sure can suck up to him the best we can,'" said Walters. "And we also thought, unless he gets a divorce, he's not going to want to put that putter down." Other Yes! models include Olivia, Tiffany, and Dianna.

Can Shania be far behind?

CHAPTER 6

The Nobility of Putting

If golf has only one thing over the other sports humans play—and it has many things, of course—it's a deep tradition of fair play and honesty that was in place even as golf became a high-stakes international sport almost 100 years ago. My father didn't play golf for the last 60 years of his life, and you didn't catch him watching it on television, either, but I remember his admiring tone when he told me how Bobby Jones more than once called a penalty on himself in a big tournament and once told an awed journalist afterward, "You might as well praise me for not breaking into banks. There is only one way to play this game." That particular penalty came in the 1926 U.S. Open, when he moved his putter next to a ball on the slope of the green and the sudden lack of breeze let the ball move about an inch.

You can argue that this was a seminal moment in the development of competitive golf. When Tom Kite called a similar penalty on himself a few years ago, he said the very same thing Jones had said, because Jones has always been the archetype for achievement, competitiveness, and fairness in golf, and he's now in the game's DNA.

Jones's most famous penalty came as he held a putter, and I'd argue that the green inspires noble behavior more than any spot on the course. Maybe it relates to what sports psychologist Larry Eimers said in chapter 1, about putting being the truest representation of a golfer's inner self—fear and guilt along with confidence and whatever else. With our souls bared and on display, golfers don't want the disgrace of cheating any more than the disgrace of a jacked four-footer.

Here's a perfect example. After a fine first round at the 2005 British Open, David Toms was troubled by the sense that his ball had moved as he was addressing it to putt—grounds for a penalty whether the golfer caused the movement or not. He talked it over with officials, and

TOEING THE LINE

Good golfers realign their ball so that the seam between the two pieces points toward the hole. This is to avoid striking the ball at the edge of a dimple, which can wreak surprising havoc on a putt. Jeff Sluman was lining up a putt this way at the 2004 Buick Classic when he noticed that the ball didn't have a side stamp, required by the USGA to confirm that the ball conforms to its regulations. It was a Titleist ProV1 that slipped though before the company employed a computerized scanner to catch such flaws. Sluman was disqualified, despite tournament officials' attempts to find a precedent that would exonerate him. The same thing happened to Greg Norman in 1996. "A severe penalty?" he asked rhetorically. "Golf has lots of severe penalties." Sluman made no excuses, either.

they all agreed there weren't grounds for a penalty. But his conscience kept working on him. Later he changed his mind, called a penalty on himself, and, since he'd signed his scorecard already, was disqualified.

"It was the right thing," Toms said later. "I was the only one who knew what happened or might have happened. . . . I told the R&A and they said, 'What if we say no harm, no foul?' I said, 'What if I come back and win this tournament or have a top-five? Or any finish?' I would've felt like I got away with something."

The American Toms had to make the long trip home early, and he may have wished he'd done what Paul McGinley did a year before at the same tournament. In the same circumstances on the very first green, McGinley called a penalty on himself. He recovered and finished the round under par.

Honesty is one facet of sportsmanship. Courtesy is another. That's why writers took Tiger Woods to task for wounding the green at the U.S. Open in 2005, dragging his putter along it as he walked off after a botched putt. "I was pissed" was one of his nonapologies, according to reports.

But Woods has been known to do the courteous thing, too. During the 36-hole final of the 2004 Accenture Match Play Championship, he gave Davis Love III a

John Sommers/Reuters

Tiger Woods drew a rebuke from the USGA after he became frustrated and damaged the ninth green at the 2005 U.S. Open. Woods is famous for his flare-ups, but he can be sportsmanlike as well.

two-foot putt on the 21st hole, while Love was dealing with heckling from a callous fan. During the heckling, Tiger also encouraged Love to take his time and regain focus. As bloodless as Tiger is supposed to be, he clearly has a heart: we saw it at the 2005 Accenture event, when John Daly missed a three-foot par putt on the second play-off hole—after missing a 15-foot birdie attempt— to lose to Woods. Tiger winced and covered his eyes as the putt veered off, and later he admitted that no one wants to win a tournament that way. There but for the grace of God went Tiger, for he'd blown some big three-footers earlier in the year.

If you want bloodless, look to Jack Nicklaus— except that Jack understood vulnerability on the green, too. He gave Tony Jacklin a putt on the final hole of the Ryder Cup in 1969 that gave England a tie after five straight Cup defeats. Reports had the putt as long as four feet—a knee-knocker—but Jacklin told authors Ron Cherney and Michael Arkush in *My Greatest Shot,* "It was between 20 and 24 inches, it wasn't a bloody four feet like some people say." In any case, Jacklin wrote to thank Nicklaus privately for the gesture shortly after- ward, and—what do you know!—the two are now col- laborating on a ritzy Bradenton, Florida, golf club called the Concession. Still, it sounds like Jacklin doesn't want

HAPPY BIRTHDAY,
MR. PRESIDENT

If a conceding a putt is the height of sportsmanship, what is asking for a concession? Presidential prerogative, apparently. John F. Kennedy, probably the best golfing president, was notorious for asking for putts. Playing with longtime friend Chris Dunphy at the Seminole Golf Club on Florida's Atlantic coast, Kennedy laced a 4-iron to within three feet of the cup. In one account, Kennedy said to Dunphy, "C'mon Chris, certainly you're not going to make me putt this." To which Dunphy replied, "Well, Mr. President, it's early in the round. Let's see what your stroke looks like today."

"Okay, fine," Kennedy said, "but let's get going. I've got a meeting with the head of the IRS right after we finish."

"It's good," said Dunphy.

the gesture to be overrated, but great golfers have missed shorter putts under less pressure, so it's reasonable that many people consider Nicklaus's concession the greatest act of sportsmanship in history.

It has some competition, though, right on the green. I'd argue that Nicklaus didn't have as much to lose (in an era when the Americans dominated the Ryder Cup and retained it, anyway, in 1969, with a tie) as Bobby Jones had in 1928, when he agreed to let the underdog Johnny Farrell putt first throughout many of the three rounds in which they were paired at the U.S. Open, in order to keep galleries from hustling to the next tee after Jones holed out. This meant Jones never had the opportunity to put pressure on Farrell with a dramatic made putt, and he must have wished later that he could have, as Farrell beat Jones by one stroke in the play-off. "It was a little disconcerting," Farrell would later recall, "so I asked Bobby if he would mind marking his ball until I finished putting. Someone else might have refused. But you know what sort of sportsman Jones was." At the 1926 Open, described earlier, Jones had had to birdie the final hole to avoid a play-off. Is there a golfer whose sportsmanship with a putter has had greater consequences?

Somehow it seems right to end with this next story,

KEEP YOUR HAT ON, CHI CHI

Chi Chi Rodriguez says his matador routine stems from a 20-foot putt he made as a kid, good for a nickel in a contest with a friend. The ball went in, then popped out, along with a toad that had been resting at the bottom of the cup. The friend insisted the putt didn't count. So Chi Chi developed the habit of tossing his wide-brimmed hat over the cup when he made an important putt, telling it symbolically to stay put. Other pros complained he was putting extra wear on the green, so then-PGA Tour commissioner Joe Dye asked him to develop another calling card. Thus his trademark matador act, in which he "re-sheaths" his putter after "slaying" the putt.

even though it's not the most dramatic. Maybe it's the most resonant. Payne Stewart's final act on the international golf stage was to concede a long putt to Colin Montgomerie on the 18th hole of the final match of the

Payne Stewart's (left) *last act on the world golf stage was to concede a putt to Colin Montgomerie at the 1999 Ryder Cup, giving the Scotsman the match and atoning for the boorish behavior of U.S. fans.*

1999 Ryder Cup, a few months before Stewart died. The Americans had already won the Cup in controversial fashion, and ugly Brookline, Massachusetts, fans had heckled the Scotsman Montgomerie throughout the tournament. Stewart's gesture was entirely appropriate—and who knows, maybe Stewart felt a little kinship with Monty, as each man had his own distinct way of rubbing people the wrong way, although Stewart tended to come away with everyone's affection. With the concession, Stewart's Ryder Cup record slipped under .500.

Now that you know a bit more about the history of sportsmanship on the green, remember this about a conceded putt. Cagey competitors will sometimes concede a short one early in the round with the idea of keeping their opponent from experiencing a confidence-boosting holed putt. In fact, this gracious act has a sinister side: the rules say you can't turn down a concession.

CHAPTER 7

Putter Reps: On the Front Lines

Noah Liberman

L ots of big, fancy, high-tech vehicles park at golf tournaments. They make the tour buses at a rock concert look like a kiddie parade.

There are the TV trucks with their antennas and satellite dishes. There's the tour's ShotLink data truck, and there's the physical therapy truck for the sore-back guys. There are motor homes belonging to players who prefer the freedom of the open road. (The 84 Lumber Classic has a black-uniformed butler stationed at its specially built motor-home park, and this butler directs each player to his parking spot, where a piping-hot apple pie and other amenities await.)

All of these buggies play key roles, but the ones that mean the most to players are, without a doubt, the "tour vans," which are actually 20-to-40-foot trucks and semi-trailers packed with the latest club-making/fixing/fitting technology and a handful of true road dogs—club technicians who spend Monday through Wednesday catering to the players' strokes and psyches and the rest of the

Noah Liberman

week migrating to the next tournament, resting, and playing golf.

"This isn't a good job if you don't like traveling," says Larry Watson, the top Titleist tour rep and Tom Watson's brother. Watson was lured back onto the road after he retired from competitive golf. He says he missed having a weekly routine built around a tournament, and he missed the camaraderie. He's on the road more than 40 weeks a year, traveling overseas as well, for major events. And the camaraderie isn't just with a couple of coworkers and the company's endorsers. Tour technicians know one another and have formed a kind of fraternity—(and fraternity's the right word, for there's not a woman to be found here). Rob Burbick is a Nike rep who happens to double as the driver of Nike's 30-foot truck. He's known on the tour as Nike Rob. "There were a lot of

Magic happens inside "tour vans" like the Titleist van at left. Here is where players come to have their putters tweaked for competition, to suit the players' strokes and restore their confidence.

The candy store: arrayed around the practice green at pro events are putter makers' latest offerings. They make for a gorgeous, colorful sight. Pros are freely encouraged to try any putter they like—so much the better if it ends up in their bags on Thursday.

guys out here named Rob for a while," he says. "I was Mizuno Rob when I worked there, then Nike Rob—it was how we kept everyone straight." Burbick's a former club pro who said he "got tired of wearing saddle shoes" and catering to members. Now he caters to guys who at least don't snap-hook six drives a round. Burbick is around 40 and has spiky bleached hair. MacGregor tour rep Robert Evans is middle-aged and weathered from sun and cigarettes. But he's like Burbick—and most of the others: outgoing, a good listener, inquisitive, optimistic. These attributes help, because these fellows have to make, adjust, and fix clubs for just about any pro who saunters by and asks for help. If you're a Nike endorser, Burbick does what you ask to your clubs, or he even makes you new ones. If you're not a Nike endorser, Burbick is still supposed to find time to make you the club you want, in case you put it in your bag that Thursday and add to Nike's "count" in the official weekly Darrell Survey. Doing well in the Darrell Survey is key for club makers, because enthusiasts pay attention and buy accordingly—just as they do when they read that so-and-so was playing with a such-and-such when he shot a 65 with 25 putts to win the this-or-that Open.

Actually, these tour reps are also a little high-strung. It's because they're competitive and they're under pressure to keep their players happy and win converts to their clubs. They're on the front lines of battle. Ask Taylor-Made's top tour rep, Byron Eder, what he'll do for a player, you get this, delivered in about 15 seconds.

"I can change the loft, lie, or grip, change the length of a putter. I can go further than that depending on the look or feel you want to achieve. We can add up to 18 grams of tungsten to bring up the swing weight. If I want to go from D-0 to D-3, I can, but if I get to D-5, then I have to grind some off the bottom. We can make it stiffer, remove a bit of [the shaft at] the bottom, move the step-down [where a narrower shaft segment starts], put the shaft back in and add an extension at the top, or take another shaft that's 40 inches long, cut it here and here, and make it stiffer, or put another shaft in there with no steps at all. If I want to cut a putter to 33 inches I can add weight with the plugs. When Sergio [Garcia, a TaylorMade endorser] won at Congressional, the putter I made for him—I made it 33 inches—I removed 6-gram weight plugs and added 14-gram weight plugs to keep the swing weight the same, and the overall length of the club was heavy enough for him to retain his feel. . . ."

Noah Liberman

Chock-full of equipment, machinery, and know-how, the TaylorMade tour van is a million-dollar rolling workshop.

Eder doesn't stop until you interrupt him. In the million-dollar TaylorMade tour van, he's in constant chatter with his colleagues, asking questions, giving orders, joking and teasing. But on the practice green, he's quieter, like all the reps. They spend a lot of time just standing next to company-logoed golf bags that brim with putters, waiting to answer questions or soft-sell a

Tour reps spend a lot of time next to the practice green looking for the chance to make the pros happy with a better putter. Yes! Golf's Jerry Walters has a computerized ball-roll analyzer to keep him company. (He also has instant messaging, to share jokes with his daughter.)

Noah Liberman

passing player. Says Callaway tour rep Jon Laws, "The player might give my putter a tiny look, maybe go 'Hmmmm,' and you think, 'Now we've got something.' The player's looking for something he already knows he wants."

Nor can the reps get uppity. That's not how you win converts. Jerry Walters, Yes! Golf's rep, made two putters for Steve Flesch, at the golfer's request. "The next time I saw him I said, 'Did you get those putters?' 'Yep'—end of conversation. I figured he tried 'em and didn't like 'em and went on to something else. About all I can do is make sure they arrived." And hope. Pro golfers rarely toss out a putter, and there's always a chance that a player will switch putters between rounds. The Darrell Survey—based on Thursday's club count—is important, but what's in the winner's bag on Sunday is more so.

Of course, by Sunday, the tour reps and club technicians are far from the action. The tour vans have to clear out by Thursday, when play starts. That's when players are on their own (or searching out local golf shops for a quick repair). By Sunday, the young techs have already driven the van to the next tour stop, and the higher-ranking veterans have spent a couple days back home and are fixing to fly to the next event. They keep an eye on television monitors in airports to see if one of their players is in contention.

Next time you're at a PGA Tour event, look for a line of 10 or 20 big trucks and trailers festooned with company logos and 10-foot-tall images of superstars and their clubs. You'll find the trucks idling near the driving range, usually. At some events, you can saunter by and peek in, and if the technicians are bored they might answer a question or give you a hat. Kids gravitate to the vans to look for discarded equipment. At one event, a 12-year-old walked up to Evans with a graphite shaft he'd scored from another company's rep and asked if Evans could put a new MacGregor driver head on it. "Can't do that," Evans said. "How much would it cost me?" the kid asked. "Three hundred dollars," Evans said. "Oh," the kid said, then shuffled off. But if the kid beats enough balls over the next decade and gets a tour card, Evans will be more than happy to make him that driver.

CHAPTER 8

The Long, Uphill Putt: Becoming a Putter Designer

Courtesy of PING Inc.

A poignant *Golf Digest* story a few years ago detailed the suffering that undiscovered putter designers endure. It painted a bleak picture. Janis Zichmanis, an advertising executive, invented the Pure Pendulum putting system: thick, tapered grips that put the hands in a prayerlike position that allowed the shoulders to remain perfectly level—an intriguing idea for anyone who's had a teacher tinker with his address. For his trouble, Zichmanis nearly lost his home, has had to borrow money from friends, and has had enough brushes with his "big break" to drive a lesser man insane.

Walt Boettger, who has pioneered a torque-controlling octagonal shaft, refinanced his house twice, the story said, and he had an income of $500 in 2002. He and his wife, Judy, would often eat just one meal a day.

Alex Gammill hit on the idea of extreme perimeter weighting and ordered 2,500 putter heads from a plant in Taiwan. The heads were supposed to arrive in 6 months, but they took 18, and by then even more radically weighted putters were on the market.

But the *Golf Digest* story included two quotes, widely separated in the piece, that together get to the truth of it. When you're on the inside, it feels easy. When you're on the outside, you need to hope, hard. A Taylor-Made product marketer said of would-be designers: "Their odds are probably better on winning the Power-ball than coming up with a good putter design. But it keeps them off the street and off the golf course, and both are good things." Snob. But Kevin Burns, who once used savings for a house to buy a milling machine in-stead, said, "That's the beauty of it—there's plenty of room for everyone. How big do I have to be to be suc-cessful?" Burns was selling about 40,000 putters a year at the time, a tiny fraction of what TaylorMade sells, and he was pretty happy about it.

Roughly 10 companies comprise 90 percent of the

U.S. putter market, and they all have their own putter-builder-in-residence, so the hopefuls have to think like Burns. In fact, many of the famous designers needed serious luck to get over the top, so the hopefuls have reason to keep faith. And, finally, putter designers come from all kinds of backgrounds, so it doesn't really matter who your daddy is or where you went to college. To prove all this, let's take a look at some designers at all levels, masters and hopefuls, with an eye toward how they got started, why they got started, and how they approach their craft.

When you survey the population of putter designers, you see lots of engineers and former engineers. And you do see some who learned at the elbows of their fathers, who were putter designers themselves. But you also find people who came to it not by way of lathes and milling machines but by way of fine art, or even something as abstract as language—words. These different backgrounds all illuminate real aspects of the putter and the challenge of designing them. But we have to start with the engineers, because the greatest putter designer of all was an engineer.

Karsten Solheim was an engineer, but it's possible he would have become a designer no matter what career he'd had, because he was so damn stubborn. That's what comes through in the fascinating biography overseen by his wife, Louise, and apparently written against his wishes. Late in his life, as he was suffering from Parkinson's disease, a writer showed up to interview him for the book, and he refused, saying, "I don't want a book written about me!" "However," Louise writes in the introduction to *Karsten's Way*, "having put my hand to the plow, I decided to see the project through." There was stubbornness on both sides of the breakfast table in that household.

Solheim had several careers. He was a brilliant national salesman for Miracle Maid cookware (but got fired anyway for having photos of the products made and selling, more efficiently, with those rather than by demonstrating the cookware); and he was the General Electric engineer who designed the first rabbit-ear antenna. In his spare time, he was an excellent athlete, the Syracuse, New York, city bowling champion, and a five-handicap golfer four years after he took up the game, at age 42. But his first experience with the futility of putting was traumatic, and he resolved then and there to create a better tool. Several years into his side career designing and selling putters, he created the Anser, which pioneered heel-toe weighting and had mechanical lines and an unusual offset that grew to look just right to

Karsten Solheim, the greatest putter designer ever, and his Anser,
still in play today.

INSCRUTABLE BEN

Does this make you feel better about your investments? Or your putter? In the summer of 2004, the financial magazine *Economist* reported on Federal Reserve Board policy thus: "Mr. [Ben] Bernanke [at that time a deputy to Fed chairman Alan Greenspan] has likened the Fed's 'gradualist' approach to that of a golfer not quite sure of his putter. Each stroke is a bit of an experiment, revealing something about the club, as well as getting the ball closer to the hole. Better, then, to make a series of tentative, 'lagged' putts, rather than risk sending the ball past the cup with one over-confident stroke. Certainly, the markets think Wednesday's putt is the first of many." The Fed's no Jack Nicklaus, is it?

millions of golfers casting around for help. ("Answer" didn't fit on the putter's sole, so the clever Louise suggested the memorable "Anser.") There is no doubt that the Anser and all of the knockoffs since its patent expired two decades ago represent the best-selling putter design ever.

Bob Bettinardi is an engineer, too, who already had a successful metal fabricating business when he saw a milled putter in a pro shop in 1990. Milled putters (shaped out of solid pieces of metal by fast-moving cutting tools) were very new at the time, as most putters were still either cast (in molds, from molten metal) or forged (shaped under heat and pressure) and required some degree of handworking for smooth surfaces. The lifetime golfer and lifetime tinkerer saw an opportunity. It took him three months to fashion his first milled putter, but within a few years he was working for Mizuno alongside another rising star, Scotty Cameron, and together they pioneered "one-piece technology," milling the putter—head and hosel both—out of one piece. Like Cameron's today, Bettinardi's sticks stand out for their subtle, very-high-quality modifications to classic designs or, increasingly, for innovative twists of their own. One of them is the futuristic Baby Ben mallet, the club Jim Furyk used in prototype to win the U.S. Open in 2003 on greens one writer described as "linoleum fast." The putter highlighted how far Bettinardi had come in 13 years. By then he had his own company, Bettinardi Golf, a deal with Hogan Golf (since ended), and a facility where both putters and high-tech defense-industry parts are made, giving him two careers at once. The Baby Ben illuminates Bettinardi's career arc in another way: he made 70 prototypes in two months before Furyk tried the putter on a Tuesday and carried it on Thursday—a testament to the powers of milling and the CNC (computer numeric control) technology Bettinardi has applied to the making of putters.

Tad Moore is yet another famous designer whose background is in engineering; he was in the castings and forgings business in the early 1960s when he made his first putter. His fabricating company made the seals for the Lunar Rover in the early 1970s, and manufacturing parts for heavy industry was his main work until 1988. A year later, Fuzzy Zoeller finished second in a tournament with a Tad Moore creation, and this helped put Moore among the design elite; at its peak in the 1990s, his company was making up to 300,000 putters a year for Maxfli and others. Zoeller didn't even know who Moore was when he used the putter that week—a feature of the looser days when players would cast around for sticks that felt good and putter brands weren't as iconic as they are today. But that's not to say Moore was a nobody, and in 1990 he made the first computer-precision-milled putter, maybe the one Bettinardi saw in that pro shop. But while Moore is proud of his fabricating milestone, he retains a deep preference for old-fashioned methods: he still makes his prototypes by hand, just as he did his first putter in 1963, a Calamity Jane–style blade that he fashioned in wood and had a vendor sandcast out of bronze for a softer feel and a bit more heft than the one Bobby Jones would have used four decades earlier. And he doesn't mince words when talking about the generational difference. "A lot of people in the last few years say they're putter makers, but they have digitized hundreds of putter [models] and they just do it on the computer," he says. "I call that modeling, copying almost and certainly not designing."

But even Moore can't match the earthiness of his friend, the famous designer T. P. Mills, who designed putters for two decades for Spalding and a few more years for Mizuno before settling back into private practice a decade ago with his son David. Mills made his reputation by hand—milling, welding, grinding, tinting, and polishing custom creations one at a time in his workshop and selling them to putter mavens at all levels of golf for $500 or more. He was the first to finish a putter head in black, for better contrast with the ball and thus better aiming. Says Moore: "T. P. Mills is a friend of mine. I watched him and I said, 'Wow, this is much too difficult. There must be a way to make machines do some of this.' " Incidentally, this led to a separate innovation of Moore's, fusion welding, in which the putter's hosel is spun in place inside the head, which fuses the pieces together permanently. But while Moore is deeply respected throughout the industry, Mills gets a special kind of reverence, for both his designs and the way they are brought to life. "No one is better than T.P. over the grinder," says Nike club

Tad Moore: an innovator with a reverence for traditional methods.

Courtesy of Tad Moore

technician Rob Burbick, who worked at Mizuno and watched Mills in his West Virginia workshop. "He can take anything he has in his head and make it happen to the steel—and then he can do it again and again."

Mills's hands-on spirit inhabits aspiring putter makers everywhere, and perhaps they can take pride in the story of Bud Allen, a pro over several decades and a friend of former pro and PGA Tour commissioner Deane Beman, but just an amateur putter maker. Barry Hyde,

T. P. Mills (right) *and his son David: decades of putter-making genius in one family.*

the USGA's chief marketing officer, tells the story about meeting Allen during a corporate golf outing in the early 1990s and receiving a call from him in his hotel room later. It seems Allen had a putter he'd made in his garage that he thought Hyde would benefit from. Hyde describes it as shaped like an elongated football and adjustable with several allen screws. Hyde remembers putting like a madman for eight months with the stick—until it drew the attention of some ne'er-do-well in the bag rack at La Costa and disappeared forever. "I tried to track another one down through his agent at the time, but [Allen] didn't have any more than the ones he'd made in his garage, just like Karsten Solheim," Hyde says.

These are the engineers and mechanics and tinkerers who represent so many putter designers at all levels. But their backgrounds suddenly seem conventional when you consider some other bona fide designers, like sculptor Robert Engman and the former ad agency executive, Janis Zichmanis, whom I mentioned earlier.

Struggling hopeful designers might fume when they read about Engman, who became a paid putter designer before he'd ever done more than tinker with a bunch of Ping Ansers in his workshop. No pro had ever used one of his sticks. Basically, only he had used his sticks. But his sculptures are in the Hirshhorn Museum and the Museum of

Modern Art, and he has been the senior champion twice at Merion Golf Club. You've heard of Merion. Fifteen years ago Engman played golf with the daughter of a man who owned a lacrosse equipment company and wanted to branch into putters, and when she saw his golf game and his home-modified Anser, she recommended him to her dad, Dick Tucker. STX Golf has the patent on an extremely soft face-insert material, and owner Tucker wanted someone who could fashion a beautiful putter around it. The insert's claim is that it doesn't deform the ball at impact, even for an instant, unlike any putter with a harder face. This makes for a truer roll, and Engman insists that if you try the putter for several rounds, you'll get used to the feel and be a convert. With the unconventionally soft insert, the rest of the putter is freed from some of the manufacturing requirements of typical putters, and so Engman's designs don't need to be milled or welded; they're cast in "trees" of 30 or 40. And this means they can have artistic lines and names like the Impressionist Series. He considers his works to be firmly in the traditions of the putters we're familiar with, but he believes his are more beautiful, which plays a huge role in confidence as you're standing over a putt. "I pay no attention to whether these things are successful in terms of proceeds, and I never alter what I'm doing in terms of how it will affect sales. Mine are whatever notion I have of beauty," he says. Before you turn up your nose, consider that Jesper Parnevik and Seve Ballesteros have used Engman designs, and Scott McCarron was using one as this book was being written. Not bad for Engman, a guy who had to familiarize himself with putter history before he could turn in his first design.

Famous sculptor Robert Engman found his way into putter design—and his STX Sync Tour, shown here, found its way into the hands of Seve Ballesteros and Jesper Parnevik.

If Engman has had it good, then Zichmanis has had it bad, although there's no saying his day won't come. Zichmanis must be one of the least likely putter innovators around, since he isn't an engineer or mechanic, and only a minor tools guy. Nor is he a great golfer, though he's not a duffer. He's an advertising creative director by training, and fittingly he created his invention in his head, leaning on a few key words and logical reasoning.

Writing and conceptualizing was Zichmanis's job, and he speaks in full paragraphs—long, long paragraphs. They're interesting; here's one.

"I've been at this full time for three and a half years, doing absolutely nothing else other than basically trying to spread the gospel of the Pure Pendulum, in a nutshell. The idea hit me December 29, 2001, that's when it happened. I spent my life—I know this is going to sound megalomaniac or melodramatic, but I mean it in a balanced sense—I really think my whole life was a prep for this particular project. The combination of the attributes it takes to make this successful, very few people would have. Basically it's a new idea, and I have spent more than 30 years in the advertising game coming up with and selling new ideas. I was a 'creative' guy. But that's my past life. I left that life. The highlights, though: in '82, I was the creative director for Coca-Cola Canada. In '90, the creative director for Budweiser Canada. For four years I was the creative director for the second largest Canadian bank. And I was always just an idea guy, not the management type. And I put up with the whole ad game for 35 years for two moments. One was when you got the goddamn idea. [Waiting for the idea] was like being paid to go to church every day. The second thing was to see the idea [become] real—when you're watching the box at home, and the damn [commercial] comes on. That transition from nothing to something again is a magical step, and that's what kept me in the ad game. On the side, I used to always play around with ideas just for the hell of it. You know what I mean; every writer, as far as I'm concerned, is a hidden megalomaniac. Now, I've been golfing for 50 years, and in 1997, I decided I'm going to learn this bloody game. I had been [shooting] in the 80s and 90s, and I have a Ph.D. in watching the Golf Channel, I swear to God. I took lessons, totally submersed myself in the game, five buckets a day, and got to a workable 13 handicap. I learned to hit the ball so I can play the course. Then what happened on that day [in 2001], I came home from Montreal and I was watching the Golf Channel as usual. They're talking about consistency, as usual. I have a carpet runner year-round on my living room floor [to practice putting], that's how bad I got the bug. I said to myself, "Okay smart guy, what's the secret of consistency in putting?" The secret is balance. And we're not talking mental balance—physical balance is the key to any physical motion. What's the secret to balance? Well, symmetry, because you can be asymmetrical and be in balance for a bit, but sooner or later you'll lose that balance. And then is when the bloody idea hit me. I thought, if that's true, and as far as I'm concerned it is true, when you're [gripping the putter] right-hand low, you're not symmetrical, in balance. So the question hit me, "Why don't we putt with thumbs level—because then the shoulders can be in balance and everything is in balance. I literally asked myself the question, 'Why don't we?' Literally, I did. So I say, 'Okay, the obvious reason we don't is because the existing grips don't allow it!'

A few months later, Zichmanis retired. "I decided, I'm going with this," he says. "I don't care if I have to sleep in a friend's basement, I don't care whose ass I have to kiss, what phone call I have to make—I had that training in advertising." So he fashioned a prototype Pure Pendulum grip out of balsa wood to get USGA approval—the grip is 1.75 inches wide, the maximum allowed—and he took his show on the road. He now has an attractive Web site that he developed, and grips and entire putters with heads designed by Clay Long, who also designed the MacGregor Response that Jack Nicklaus used in his famous Masters win in 1986. He has appeared in magazine feature articles touting the system, he has the informal blessing of a top golf-magazine edi-

Janis Zichmanis won't give up until his Pure Pendulum system is in your hands.

tor who liked the putter after Zichmanis talked his way into the man's office, he has laboratory proof that his system promotes balance and consistency in the stroke, and he's sold his wares (a few hundred units in all) in 28 U.S. states and 8 Canadian provinces. He knows the only thing he lacks is demand for his product, but any adman worth his salt believes he can generate that, if given the resources. "The missing link is money," Zichmanis says. "I've been looking since [the summer of 2004] for money." One New York billionaire showed significant interest, kept him waiting for an answer, then begged off, saying the project wasn't big enough. Another investor made him a satisfactory offer right on the phone, then disappeared for two weeks, during which he had emergency bypass surgery. There have been others, but as of this writing, Zichmanis says,

"We're right, totally, on the cusp. As we speak I am waiting to get resolutions on two financial situations. . . . What I'm after is, I want to revolutionize putting, create a whole new putting category. That's the part that kills me that I can't understand, why they can't pick up on it."

At this point, you're having one of a few reactions. You may be relieved that you aren't inclined to invent putters. Or you may have decided it's time to stop trying. Or you may have just decided you, too, are going to give it a whirl. Good luck to you. But if you're a famous putter designer already, here's hoping I've given you renewed respect for your good fortune and for the efforts of those who haven't reached your level yet. They've got every right to be on the street—and on the golf course.

Even this fellow does. T.P. and David Mills heard a knock on the door of their studio many years ago. "We had a gentleman come through here, and as all who do, he had the next best thing in putters," David says. "After the situation was all over, we thought maybe he wasn't all there. At least it seemed that way. He had a putter shaft with a piece of lead on it. We asked him what he thought was so great. He said you could never miss a putt with it. We asked how. He said the way this lead hits the ball, it makes it spin back into the cup if you hit it past the hole."

CHAPTER 9

Putter Marketing: Science? Smoke and Mirrors? Do We Care?

Wherever you go, they're marketing putters to you. When you're on the course, they're marketing. When you're in a golf store, they're marketing. They're marketing to you in magazines and on TV, even when you're not watching the commercials. They're even marketing when you sleep, because somewhere there's a putter company making its designers, marketers, copywriters, and lawyers figure out how they're going to persuade you to buy their putter when you wake up.

And you know what? You probably will. Putters are nearly a $200 million business at retail in the United States alone—more than a million and a half sticks a year—and the worldwide numbers are many times as large. So to keep selling new putters at that clip, putter makers have to convince you that you need a new putter. That is, they need to market hope.

Actually, the hope is already in you, because no one is ever entirely happy with his or her putting. Putter companies have to play to this hope and convince you that their putters are better than the one in your bag and the four dozen in your basement. They do this partly by searching for better, more effective designs—through science. But science only gets them so far. (For proof, reach chapter 3 and see that there have been fewer than a dozen truly revolutionary putter designs ever.) So they turn to marketing. "The putter business is 5 percent science and 95 percent marketing," says an executive with a well-known golf-club manufacturer. And he is not the lone voice of truth. "Putters are a little bit science, and a lot of smoke and mirrors," says a longtime golf-equipment executive.

Neither one sounds guilty, either, and that's okay, because deep down we all know the score. We know that the next putter we buy is not likely to be the last, but it might be fun for a while. So there must be a peculiar pleasure in the purchase itself, in the hoping. It might just be that the best part of a putter is the short drive home from the store, while the putter is still sitting next to you in the passenger seat, promising the world. If you can acknowledge that, you'll be amused to discover all the ways that the putter company contrived to get you to buy its putter.

It starts in their workshop, where designers are working on two tracks at once. On one, they're looking for the next revolutionary design—but they know that's an unlikely find. "That's the $50 million dollar question," says Tom Olsavsky, director of product creation at TaylorMade, which markets the Rossa putter line, fourth most popular among consumers, according to the last full-year Darrell Survey, done in 2004. "In many cases we see designs and shapes we like, but we just don't know what to expect." On the other track, they're working on some little tweak—a new finish, a slightly different offset—that fires your desperate imagination. "If you don't have something new every year, you're out of business," says Pat Sellers, national sales manager for SeeMore Golf, who knows whereof he speaks. A SeeMore was in Payne Stewart's hands when he won the 1999 U.S. Open at Pinehurst, and the company reached $6 million in sales a year later, great for a small shop. But by 2004, when Sellers was hired by investors as "the only employee—janitor, designer, phone-answering man, Web designer," he says, the company was down to $85,000 in sales. It's now back up to roughly $550,000, thanks to fresh designs, and 26 different pros used its putters at some point in 2005.

The fact is, as much as golfers of all kinds want a revolution in their hands, they're also conservative and hesitant to buy putters that look or feel too different. "We have some putters that are still in the research-and-design closet and work better than a lot of putters out here but just don't look right," says Olsavsky. That's why TaylorMade has its most promising designs worked over and made more visually appealing by an outside firm, Priority Designs of Columbus, Ohio, which has done similar work for companies as diverse as Carrier (the air-conditioning people) and American Standard (the faucet people). The interchangeable TLC weights in both Tay-lorMade's Rossa Monza Corza putter and its r7 drivers? Priority Designs tweaked them to look sleeker and more high-tech.

This sounds a bit superficial, but if it is, then so is the entire game of golf, because even the best players in the world are influenced by a club's looks. After Vijay Singh changed putters and lapped the field at the 2005 Buick Open, he explained, "I was tired of looking at one

Payne Stewart wasn't the only one jubilant with the putting that earned him the 1999 U.S. Open. That's a SeeMore putter in his left hand, and the victory launched the company to prominence—for a while. Then it crashed. It is now making a comeback, with updated designs, like the Money (inset).

No accident: TaylorMade hired an outside industrial design firm to make sure that the interchangeable TLC weights in the back of its Rossa Monza Corza putter looked sleek and high-tech. Golfers care about this kind of thing.

putter." For Singh, the new look worked. Here's another example. The most popular putter designer today, Titleist's Scotty Cameron, is called Xerox Man by jealous competitors because many of his most famous designs are tweaks of putters originating with Karsten Solheim, T. P. Mills, and John Reuter. But Cameron's tweaks—in materials, machining, finish, balance, sound, and feel—are precisely what the pros ask for. Great putters like Tiger Woods and Brad Faxon swear by his putters—and between them have a combined 20 years with their current putters. And merely good putters credit him, too. Peter Jacobsen, who, impressively, has won on both the Champions Tour and the PGA Tour in the past few years, uses a Cameron model based on the venerable Acushnet Bulls Eye. "But Scotty takes the extra time with players to design exactly what a player wants," Jacobsen says. "I'm at his studio three or four times a year, and I'm twice as good a putter as on my early days on the tour. I think Scotty has an understanding of what I'm doing with my stroke, number one, and that's renewed and increased my confidence. When I have a 5- or 10-footer under pressure, subconsciously I say, 'I have a pretty good sense of how to make this,' but when we were pulling old drivers and putters and wedges out of barrels in my early days, you just prayed you had the right club in your hand."

Earlier in this book I quoted former pro Gay Brewer: "Putting is 90 percent mental. If you think you can't putt, you can't." What he said is not so different from what the executive said earlier. The 95 percent of putter design that's marketing partly overlaps the 90 percent of golf that's mental. Or as top putter designer Bob Bettinardi puts it, "Our business is to sell confidence. Business is good."

Now that we know what goes on behind closed doors at putter companies worldwide—and that we don't mind—let's look a little closer at the other places they're marketing to you. How about at actual tournaments? There's a reason Scotty Cameron is so good to Peter Jacobsen, apart from their both being nice guys. If Jacobsen wins a tournament, and you're a little unhappy with your putter, you notice what putter he used. And since his 5-to-10-footers look a lot like yours, you can imagine his putter working for you. Big putter companies bank on this, and small ones pray for it. When Nick Price won the 1994 PGA Championship with the odd-looking Bobby Grace Fat Lady Swings mallet, Grace had 25,000 orders immediately and was able to graduate from making putters in his garage. But he still put the space to good use: "I went from a Toyota to a Lexus overnight," Grace said—and on to a deal with Cobra and now MacGregor.

There are lots of great stories like Grace's. SeeMore had its breakthrough in 1999 when Stewart sank three astonishing putts to win that U.S. Open—in fact, the company's fast growth was one factor in its subsequent near collapse. Odyssey's White Hot 2-Ball was just another odd-looking new mallet when Paul Lawrie used one to sink a stunning 60-foot putt on the final hole of the 2001 Dunhill Links Championship, traversing the "Valley of Sin" at the 18th green at the Old Course at St. Andrews to do it. To add to the serendipity for Odyssey, it was the popular Scotsman's first win since the 1999 British Open, and it came late in the year, when golfers worldwide were starved for some interesting news. The putt got play in all the media, the more so because the 2-Ball was such an unconventional-looking beast. So there was a huge demand for the putter before Callaway Golf had spent a dime on advertising, and as the putter quickly secured the top spot in overall sales—which it still holds—the company spent a total of $400,000, one-third of what it would usually take a major company to get just "normal" results from a putter, according to Larry Dorman, Callaway Golf's senior vice president for global public relations. "All this happened because Paul Lawrie made that putt," he says.

Now how did Lawrie happen to have a 2-Ball in his

That's Paul Lawrie down there in the Valley of Sin on the 18th hole of St. Andrews's Old Course. He's celebrating the birdie putt that won him the 2001 Dunhill Links Championship. The spectacular putt won him $800,000—exactly what the ensuing publicity saved Callaway Golf in advertising expenses when the company started marketing the new White Hot 2-Ball Lawrie used to make the putt.

hand in the first place? In previous chapters, I have covered all the ways club companies bend over backward to get players to use their sticks. But in addition to the gymnastics, some companies simply pay players. And it's a curious economy. Top players are the least likely to have putter-endorsement deals, because despite being great, many of these players are fickle or even neurotic about their putters, and there's no way a club maker could pay them enough to stick with one brand when they're already switching putters at a whim and making millions of dollars on the course. In fact, there are some famous cases of players "taking the money" from a new club maker and suffering, as when Stewart switched from Wilson to Spalding in 1994 for a huge contract, but had so much trouble adjusting to cast blades, offset irons, and a two-piece ball that he plummeted from sixth on the money list to 123rd in one year. Corey Pavin and Lee Janzen have suffered similarly. But while players are generally immune to endorsement mistakes, lesser players may not be. Sellers tells a story about a pro who has one tour win, with a SeeMore, but insists on using a top maker's putter for the $1,500 a week he gets—even though he admitted to Sellers the SeeMore shaves three strokes from his score. "I went in and got a newspaper from the men's room. He had made $9,700, tied for last. Three shots better was worth

$29,000. Who cares about $1,500 when you can make $20,000 [more]? He said, 'Then you should pay me.' I thought, 'Are you that stupid?' "

The story sounds far-fetched, but it's true that players like to know there's a little extra money coming in every week, and that they're in the stable of a famous putter company. So it's the bottom half of the PGA Tour where putter endorsements predominate—usually at around $800 to $1,500 a week for maybe 20 weeks a year, giving the player the freedom to switch around a little bit. The deals help a putter maker increase its standing in the Darrell Survey. It pays even to have marginal pros using your putter, because they increase your "count," the same as the top pros do. And sometimes these guys actually do win tournaments. SeeMore paid Vaughn Taylor $50,000 for winning the Reno-Tahoe Open in 2004—actually, SeeMore's insurance company did. The club maker had a policy in case Taylor won. "So it really cost me nothing," Sellers says, since increased sales of the putter offset the cost of the policy. Taylor finished 36th on the money list in 2005, thanks to a repeat Reno-Tahoe victory, so policies on him are going to get more expensive.

These are great examples of on-course marketing. But what if someone using a company's putter doesn't win the tournament in jaw-dropping fashion, or at all?

The company still has many other ways of marketing to you through the players. Logos on bags and hats and golf shirts are a familiar one, but some newer ways have cropped up. Grips and clubfaces are two. About five years ago, a handful of companies realized that putter grips don't have to be black or dark brown. Previously, Ping's grips, with the white "PING" logo running vertically, were as radical as the marketing got. Now many of the top companies have signature colors and designs—Yes!'s bumblebee colors, Bettinardi's cool green, Taylor-Made Rossa's bold red and black—and their makers constantly tweak even these. SeeMore's see-through grips have 300 tiny dollar signs visible inside, and in 2006 they'll all be the same green as real greenbacks, at the suggestion of affable tour pro Fred Funk, a SeeMore user. In Japan it's a yen symbol inside a red circle of the flag, and a Korean-currency grip is in the works. In Europe it's still the British pound, so as not to force Britons to accept the euro sooner than they're ready, Sellers says.

You can bet these colorful grips show up on television, but they're not all that does. With the advent of the "worm cam," the angle that puts the viewer face-to-face with the putter head, companies can now show off the fancy milling they do on the putter face. Bettinardi's "honeycomb" milling pattern is done for precision flat-

Buzz: the bumblebee-colored grips on Yes! Golf's putters leave a memorable impression. Most putter makers have signature grip colors now.

ness, says Bob Bettinardi, but it also shows up nicely on the worm cam. When commentator Gary McCord noticed it on camera in 1999, he quipped, "The face looks like the parquet floor of the Boston Garden"—a comment likely to gain respect among sports fans. And if you notice that pattern on-screen, you'll remember it when you're in the pro shop or in the golf megastore.

And you'll get marketed to there, as well. Putters represent between 5 and 8 percent of the typical golf chain's revenues, less than you might expect. (Driver purchases are "testosterone-driven," according to Sven Kessler, vice president of retail sales for the large Edwin Watts chain, and they represent roughly 20 percent of his chain's revenues.) Edwin Watts calls its in-store putting centers "corrals," not because they suspect you think like a farm animal but because between 500 and 800 putters are herded into these artificial greens, which feature four to six holes. The putters are raised 30 inches off the floor so that the colorful grips are closer to eye level, and by manufacturers' request, they're now grouped by company, not price point, to take advantage of the grip-color associations and to make it easier for a customer to decide to spend just a little bit more on a company's better model. Kessler says fully half of his customers buy on brand—proof of the power of image marketing—and this was borne out by a large *Golf World Business* study of golfers and retailers a few years ago.

And the study uncovered even more slightly irrational behavior. Almost half of the golfers surveyed said they make a final decision on the basis of feel, more than three times as much as on the next feature, performance. Even top marketers who play golf fall prey to this reasoning. Carl Rose Jr., president of the large Carl's

Golfland stores outside Detroit, started selling the Heavy Putter in 2005. The stick is nearly twice as heavy as the average putter, and it notched its first pro tour win in 2005, when Troy Matteson used it in the Nationwide Tour's Virginia Beach Open. Rose decided to stock it after he himself sank 10 straight 10-footers at the PGA Merchandise Show early in 2005. But does he use it himself? "I don't have it in my bag, I probably should," he says. "It's got to kind of make sense to the customer. . . . I don't play that much golf personally. . . . I have a putter I've been with a while, and they say if [two putters are] somewhat comparable, then don't change—but we're all guilty [of doing things for] no particular reason."

Golfsmith's largest stores have 1,000-square-foot indoor greens, made with the latest in artificial turf technology and painstakingly landscaped to mimic the slopes and curves of championship-caliber greens. "We have a firm philosophy that our stores should be interactive," says Mick McCormick, senior vice president of marketing for the nationwide chain. "The only way to like a putter is to try it." But here's another bit of irrationality the *Golf World Business* survey uncovered: two in five golfers said they would buy a putter without trying it. They must be walking directly from their TVs to their computers to place those orders online—more reason for club makers to keep the pros happy and for the chains to make their Web sites pretty. "A lot of Internet shoppers want the latest and greatest, and they will buy right there," says Kessler. "The Yes! and Guerin Rife putters [two young companies with the respect of tour pros] have done really well on our homepage."

So we're all in on the irrationality game. We must be, if things like this happen: "**The** dead-on-accurate-send-it-into-the-heart-of-the-cup-fist-pumping-sultan-of-the-short-grass **Patent**." In addition to contending for the record for the longest hyphenated noun phrase in history, this bit of ad copy promotes the "interchangeable vision strips" on Callaway Golf's I-Trax putter. You can choose between straight lines or a chevron pattern and install the strip that suits your vision best. Since the 2-Ball's advent, sighting aids have become a hot marketing tool backed with some validity, as even top pros suffer from chronic aimline problems. But read the ad copy! It seems to make huge, important claims, yet it's clearly absurd and comical, and it's perfectly legal. It's what admen—and the law books—call "puffery": you know it's not literally true, but you can't help but hope it sort of is, especially since it's fun to read in the bargain. Fact, fiction, bluster, and humor: could there be a better reflection of putters and putting, or of golfers, or of golf itself?

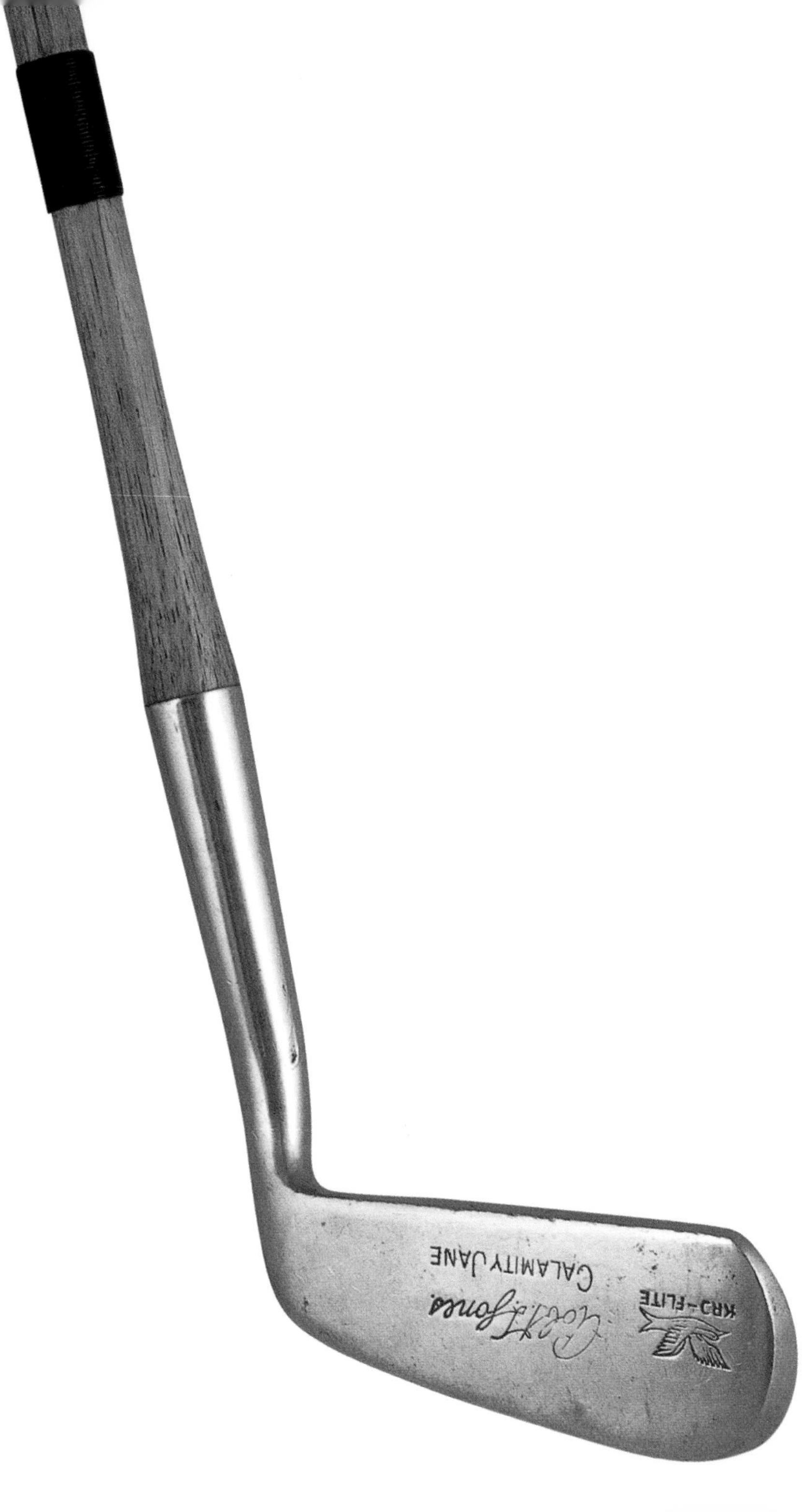
CALAMITY JANE
KRO-FLITE

CHAPTER 10

Just Like a Putter: The Rise and Fall of the Collectibles Business

The entire collectible business is dead," growls Robert Kent, owner of House of Forged, a rare-and-vintage golf-club business in San Diego. Kent's assessment is about as dire as you'll hear (how can you get worse off than dead?), but every serious golf-club collector on earth would agree that the business is nothing like it was 10 years ago. If you're a longtime serious collector or vendor, this isn't a good thing, because you probably expected your collection to be worth a lot more now than it is, even if it is, nevertheless, worth more than you paid for it.

If you're a novice, you came to the party at

a good time. You might not see your eventual collection appreciate the way collectors did between the early 1980s, when the hobby took off, and the late 1990s, when it hit its peak. The world knows too much about golf clubs now—which are rare, which aren't—and so there's less of the misinformed snarfing there was back then. But if you do some informed snarfing, you can build a pretty nice collection of collection-worthy clubs—putters included—right now.

If you've got a lot of money, like billionaire Bolivian tin magnate Jaime Ortiz-Patiño, you could have spent around $130,000 on a beautifully preserved 1850s long-nose putter that had been in the collection of Old Tom Morris, the British Open Champion and St. Andrews's first official greenskeeper in the late 1800s. Ortiz-Patiño bought the stick at auction in 2005 and will house it in the museum at the famous Spanish golf club Valderrama—which he also owns. The putter will go nicely with the early metal-blade putter he bought for $174,900 nearly a decade ago—still the highest known price paid for a flat stick.

If your tastes are a bit more economical, you can buy an official 1930s Spalding Kro-Flite Bobby Jones Calamity Jane putter for around $250. It would have cost you $500 or $600 ten years ago. Or you can just troll eBay

By permission of Zephyr Productions, Inc.

From Old Tom Morris to Jaime Ortiz-Patiño, this mid-1800s longnose putter appreciated by $130,000.

COLLECTORS' STORIES

Former pro Kel Devlin, now a Nike Golf marketer, tells how he was playing in a pro-am, and an amateur (these are usually corporate executives who have paid for the privilege of making lousy shots in the company of pros) told him he was sick of his putter, an early "Scottsdale" Ping, so-called because Ping's first generation was produced in Scottsdale, Arizona, not Phoenix as now. "I haven't been able to putt with this for 10 years," the golfer said. Devlin recognized it as a collector's item, and told the guy it was valuable. The guy wouldn't believe him and insisted he take it. "Just buy me a new one in the pro shop," he said. Devlin acquiesced, and bought him a $60 Ray Cook (now available at Play It Again Sports for $19), and has a collectible worth hundreds at his home right now.

But Devlin's a piker compared to folks like Gerald Hall, the longtime pro at Santa Ana Country Club in California, who had collected more than 60 replicas of the putters used to win the U.S. Open. He would write letters and cajole the pros into sending him exact copies of the putters, although in a few cases he wouldn't reveal, they actually sent him the originals. He discovered fascinating things about putters and their owners, such as that Andy North had wrapped medical gauze tape around the grip of the 1930s Cash-In that he used in 1985 to win the Open. And that Tiger Woods's Titleist Scotty Cameron putter had a grip from a rival putter maker—Ping—and so Woods had to black out the large Ping logo on the putter.

and find the same kind of putter you used as a teenager—maybe an Acushnet Bulls Eye or a Ping Anser or a T. P. Mills TPM 2 and pay between $10 and $40 for it.

Painful as it has been for some, the deflating of the golf-club collectibles market is an interesting story. It reflects many interesting realities in the golf world—and in the world itself.

For starters, golf-club companies don't market themselves by playing up their histories anymore. At least the successful ones don't. Until the early 1990s, Spalding, Wilson, MacGregor, Hogan, and others would woo you by reminding you that Bobby Jones or Gene Sarazen had played their clubs and that the current offerings retained significant features from those days. "Their catalogues used to say, 'In our great tradition . . . ,'" Robert Kent says. Today, that's the last thing a golfer wants to hear. Remember the message of chapter 9? It's all about being revolutionary today. So a significant catalyst has disappeared: golfers who believed a 20-year-old set of forged blades or a butter-soft Bulls Eye was truly better equipment and were eager to buy them now that they could afford them, unlike in high school.

This results-oriented nostalgia was best embodied in Japanese golfers 15 years ago. When Jumbo Ozaki was putting lights-out with a vintage MacGregor Tommy Armour IMG 5 Iron Master blade, his fans *and* his competition wanted that club. Collector and putter designer Tim Janiga remembers buying one for $50 at a pawn shop and selling it for $1,800 that same day. "Now you could find one in new condition for $600, maybe $800, and one in fair condition for $300 or less," Janiga says. "An Arnold Palmer [Wilson] 8802—I saw mint ones with Macy's price tags on them go for $10,000 15 years ago, and now you might get lucky and get $1,500." If you recall, the Japanese had a love for anything American then—jeans, music, and so on—and while it hasn't dis-

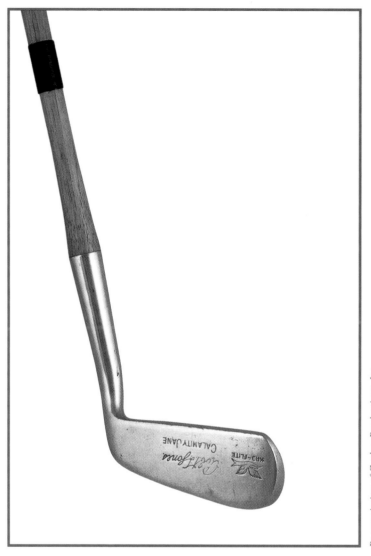

This Calamity Jane copy can be had for $250 today—from someone who paid twice as much 10 years ago.

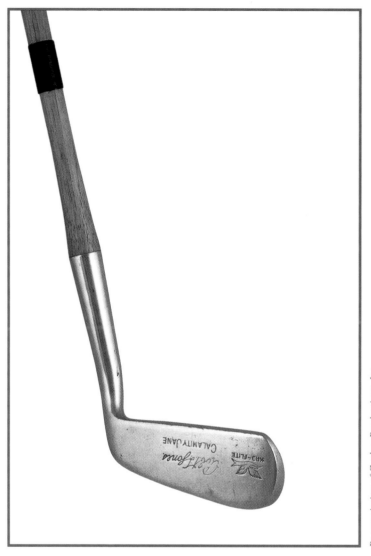

By permission of Zephyr Productions, Inc.

appeared, it's certainly not strong enough to drive the collectible-putter market anymore.

If traditional American clubs aren't lighting fires anymore, what is? The latest offerings from Scotty Cameron, Bob Bettinardi, Bobby Grace, Tad Moore, Kevin Burns, and others—many of them still young-buck putter makers with a whole lifetime of designs ahead of them, which means their collectors better keep their jobs. Most of these designers are aligned with major club companies today, and their latest retail designs go for between $150 and $600. These designers have created an interesting market dynamic. At the same time that they're coming out with new models each year, they're also coming out with collector's editions, commemorating big tournament wins by their top endorsers or even their own favorite past designs. Collectors are buying all of this stuff. "The modern-day putter makers have become celebrities," Kent says. This is very true in Japan: Bettinardi made putters under the Hogan aegis until recently, and his contract with the company allowed him to sell special lines in Japan on his own. "All the limited editions have ruined things," said one top collector, who asked not to be identified. "And you have to be the designer's fair-haired boy to get in on some of them, and it's too much work."

THE PREZ'S COLLECTIBLE

President George W. Bush ordered Scotty Cameron putters with the presidential seal milled into the clubface as part of the goody bags given to special guests at his first inauguration, in 2001. As *Golf Digest* explained, "Bush may have downplayed his passion for golf during the presidential campaign, but he couldn't keep it buried forever."

Now, you don't have to be anyone's fair-haired boy to buy old clubs online. The brilliance of the Internet—how it links huge groups of like-minded people together for the amazingly efficient transfer of goods and information—has been a blow to the golf-collectibles industry, because it made everyone aware of exactly how little is rare and how much is commodity. "People are pulling stuff out of their garages, they send their friends to thrift stores, then swap meets, then used sporting goods stores, estate sales on Thursdays, then the thrifty ads on Friday—and put it all on eBay on Saturday," Kent complains. "As opposed to clubs being in some collector's vault and nobody being able to see them."

Well, one collector's misfortune is another's bounty. Ten years ago, casual collectors were complaining about the superheated market. "I lament what has happened to the hobby of golf club collecting," wrote *Golfweek* columnist James Achenbach. "In too many ways, the average person has been jettisoned from the pastime. Prices have soared more drastically than the tournament scores of Ian Baker-Finch." The Achenbachs have to be happy today, however, because it's a wide-open marketplace. You can start a collection relatively cheaply—and intelligently, thanks to the painful knowledge gained in the past decade. And if you collect not to resell but for the love of clubs, or for the love of playing with vintage clubs of any era, as many collectors do, then a world awaits.

And there are even some collector-dealers who are bullish on the market as a long-term investment. "[Collectors] will come back, because this is still a new field in the collecting world," says David Levine, one of the top collectors in the United States today and coauthor of *The Art of Putters: The Scotty Cameron Story*. He believes interest in vintage clubs will revive as a consequence of the current interest in contemporary club makers. Collectors will mature and develop an affection for the charming clubs of the 1920s and earlier. "Most collectors who collect steel-shafted clubs end up collecting hickories," he says.

So maybe the putter collectibles market will come back. Maybe interest in certain types of putters will fill collectors with hope and confidence and they'll plunk down their money with happy hearts. The history of putter collecting has been very much like our experience with the putter itself: it goes well for a while, then it goes bad, then it goes well again. And as long as there's another putter to buy and another foursome being arranged, we're happy to join the game.

CHAPTER 11

Fifty Ways To Leave
Your Putter

John O'Boyle/Newark Star-Ledger

Truthfully, Paul Simon's tune didn't last long enough to list 50, and neither will this chapter. But you'll be amazed at the ways in which pro golfers have parted company with their putters. You might forget a 7-iron at the far end of the green after a lousy chip, or bend it by accident on tree limb, but you'd never come up with most of these wacky, anguished, theatrical breakups. It's because you don't really have a relationship with your 7-iron. It's just a tool. But your putter is your partner—until it does you wrong and you kick its butt out. Here's how the pros do it.

The Water Toss. (This is a real-life take on the golf [sub]urban legend about the golfer who tossed his clubs in the water, stalked off, returned, waded in for his car keys, then tossed the bag back. I'm sure this actually happened, but a suspicious number of people claim it happened to "a friend of a friend.") At the 2003 Australian PGA Championship, John Daly heaved his putter into the lake after a second-round 78. This round was also marred by a disagreement with a scoring official on the 13th hole and his refusal to sign his scorecard, which got him disqualified. He wasn't invited back for the 2004 event. (Apparently, lakes are just an inviting way to snuff out a putter. PGA Tour pro Ken Green parted with a putter that way several years ago, and later explained, "It was time for it to die.")

The Head Ache. Think of this the next time a putter company makes a claim for an epoch-making, patent-pending, high-technology innovation: sometimes the head just falls off. Harrison Frazar's MacGregor lost its head midround a few years ago, forcing him to putt with a 3-wood. He made three birdies over the final seven holes and followed up with a 64 the next day using an exact replica MacGregor had already made him. (Lucky for Harrison; once play starts on Thursday, players can't get any help from the official equipment technicians who

John Daly (trust us) putts with his L-wedge at a late-2005 tournament.
The head of his MacGregor putter had fallen off, again. "Ninth time this
year. I'm sick of this!" he fumed later.

stay so busy puttering with their clubs from Monday to Wednesday.) If this deheading sounds unlikely, consider that it happened at least nine times to Daly (a lightning rod for disaster) in 2005.

One time was during the first round of the WGC American Express Championship, where he bogeyed the last two holes of the first round to fall back into a tie for first. He immediately stomped off into the parking lot. "Ninth time this year. I'm sick of this," he told a reporter. The misfortune haunted him, too. He ended up tied with Tiger Woods after 72 holes, and lost the playoff two holes later when he lipped out a three-footer (with a perfectly good putter) to complete a three-putt from 12 feet—one of the most astonishing and heartbreaking finishes of any round ever. True to his theatrical nature, Daly then tried a new way of getting rid of his putter: *the Fan Donation*. He walked to the gallery and handed it to a spectator named Frank Lopez. If Frank Lopez is a true golfer, who understands the heartbreak of a missed putt, he'll never sell the putter—valuable as it is—because it embodies golf and it embodies Daly. As *Golf Digest* columnist Ron Sirak put it, "It would have been too much of a fairy tale for Daly to beat Woods, and too much out of keeping with the path his life has followed."

The Bag-Bend. At the Mercedes Championship in 2003, defending champion Sergio Garcia lost his cool and wedged his putter into his bag, bending the shaft just enough to make it "nonconforming." (The USGA has a million finicky rules about putters; when you bend a shaft midround, you've just ran afoul of one of them.) So Sergio putted with an assortment of clubs to finish that round—a fairway wood, an 8-iron, a sand wedge—and finished the round roughly 600 strokes off the pace. He got a Wilson belly putter from his dad to play the week-

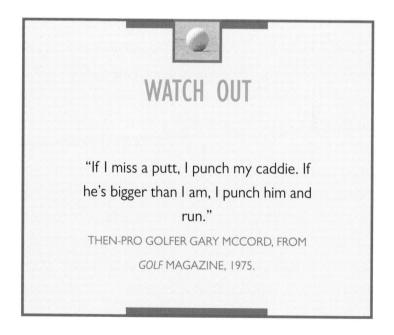

WATCH OUT

"If I miss a putt, I punch my caddie. If he's bigger than I am, I punch him and run."

THEN-PRO GOLFER GARY MCCORD, FROM

GOLF MAGAZINE, 1975.

end rounds, and continued to scuffle. He wasn't meant to defend that title. (There's a corollary to the Bag-Bend, and that's *the Knee-Break*. When you bring your putter shaft down over your knee, you're not leaving anything to chance: you want it gone. Mark McNulty did this to his putter at the 1979 Japanese Open, going a little berserk after a clumsy fan distracted him twice, once while trying to find a seat in the grandstand, then moments later when he dropped his lunchbox (yes, a lunchbox) as McNulty putted. McNulty beheaded his putter rather than the fan, then putted with his 1-iron on the way to a 77.

The Golfer's Choice. Early in 2004, Mike Weir was having putting troubles he later attributed to not keeping his lower body still during his swing. (Did you know you can move your rump enough to knock a putt off target?) During one round of the Bob Hope Chrysler Classic, Weir abandoned his putter altogether. He pulled out a sand wedge and immediately sank a 15-foot eagle putt. Actually, the sand wedge is probably the most common replacement for the putter, with its short shaft and heavy head and lots of weight low and back, thanks to the big sole. But for proof of the pros' agility, note that they still have to strike the ball just right on the thin leading edge of the club. Try it and see if you don't pop the ball up or top it. (Practice it if you plan to trash your putter during a tournament.)

The Blame-Junior. Jack Nicklaus can win tournaments with his son on the bag, but they're the Nicklauses, for Pete's sake. Mitch Voges, U.S. Amateur champ in 1992, was playing the first round of the U.S. Open that year and discovered that his son, Christian, had left his putter leaning against a watercooler at the previous tee—540 yards back. Playing partners Ian Baker-Finch and Payne Stewart were already chipping and lining up putts, respectively, so there was no way to send the absentminded son back for the putter, which David Duval was waving in the air back at the tee. (At least the goofy family was in famous company that day.) So on national TV, Voges holed a snaky 15-footer with his 3-wood. He also earned *Golf Digest*'s putt of the year award.

The Sister's Keeper. Again, if you're a big-time golfer, you need a caddy whose toothbrush didn't share space with yours in the family bathroom. LPGA pro Barb Thomas three-putted the ninth hole during a tough round about a decade ago and theatrically jammed her putter into a trash can on the way to the 10th tee. She assumed her brother "Speedy" saw her. He didn't. By the time they discovered the miscommunication, a fan was hustling the putter toward the parking lot. "She was very humbled by that," says Alice Miller, a touring pro at the time and now an LPGA tournament director. "We never let her live that down, and her brother was very disgusted with her. She was a good putter who was having a bad day."

AMATEUR THROWS PRO TANTRUM

Please don't think the pros are the only ones supremely skilled at ditching a putter. Amateurs can be quite spectacular, too. Tantrum-prone college basketball coach Bobby Knight might have pulled off the best breakup ever. He was playing the Indiana University Golf Course in 1982 when he blew a putt on the fifth hole and tossed his club in the air. It got stuck in a maple tree. Early the next morning, he climbed into the tree, but he couldn't retrieve the club. To add insult, he had to stay in the tree an extra hour to avoid being seen by other golfers.

The Practical Joke. Nick Price told *Golf Digest* a terrific story about a gag played on Mark McNulty more than 20 years ago by top jokester Simon Hobday. McNulty's a terrific putter, and his prize stick then was a 1970s-model Acushnet Bulls Eye with a blue grip. Price and McNulty were playing Hobday and Dale Hayes in an exhibition, and Hobday saw a putter like McNulty's in the pro shop, bought it, and switched it for the real thing in McNulty's bag while he wasn't looking. Soon after, at the first tee in front of 2,000 people, Hayes introduced McNulty. "You know him for his incredible putting prowess," he said. At this, McNulty demanded, "Where is that bloody putter?" He stalked over to Hobday's bag, yanked out the putter, and broke it over his knee. Said Price, "McNulty's eyes almost fell out of his head. . . . He was going to start going after Simon. There was a good 30-second period where he was in shock."

The Trust-a-Friend. Jack Nicklaus has almost every club he used in winning a major. Byron Nelson has none of them, not from any tournament he played in. One reason is that he trusted his best friend on the tour, Harold "Jug" McSpaden. After he retired, Nelson agreed to lend his Spalding Harry Cooper putter to Jug, despite misgivings. The putter was a Calamity Jane–style blade with very soft head—easily bent. Mc-

Spaden was a compulsive tinkerer, "always jacking clubs around, bending them," as Nelson put it. Nelson lent the putter on the condition that McSpaden not tinker, but he did, and in two months the head was broken. But "he was a good enough friend to name his first boy after me," the gentlemanly Nelson said, "so I couldn't get too mad at him."

ON THE OTHER HAND...

In 2003, *Golf World* asked the glamorous and controversial LPGA golfer Jan Stephenson, "Is it true you used to sleep with your putter?" She answered, "I used to take my putter to my hotel room, and people would tease me. 'Are you going to bed with it?' I'd say 'Absolutely.' I don't have kids, so golf is my love. It's everything to me. I guess I never had the golden touch in bed, with my men or my putter. But I'm working on it, and I'm getting better—with my men and my putter."

The Putter Thief (and a poignant epigraph). Ben
Crenshaw used his Wilson 8802 blade putter, which he
called Little Ben, from the age of 16 until well into his
brilliant career. (I wrote of how the putter got its name in
chapter 5.) But it wasn't with him for his first 1992 Western Open win—proof that a putter might make a golfer
better, but it can't make him great. Crenshaw was using
his manager's putter at the Western because someone had
stolen his entire bag out of his car while it was parked in
his own Austin, Texas, driveway. Three weeks later the
bag was discovered in a vehicle at a drive-in liquor store
30 miles south of town. Lucky Ben. But in a larger sense,
Crenshaw's relationship with Little Ben had been troubled for five years by then. In the middle of a 1987 Ryder
Cup round, Crenshaw three-putted the sixth at Muirfield
Village, and stalked off the green holding Little Ben by
the head, something he never did. He took a swing, shaft
first, at a buckeye on the ground, and the shaft snapped.
The buckeye was an ironic coincidence, because Ohio
State alum Jack Nicklaus was the U.S. team captain, and
moments later Crenshaw had to admit to Jack that he'd
whacked his putter with 12 holes to go. God bless Nicklaus; he just said, "Well, the way things are going, I don't
blame you." Crenshaw finished the round with sand
wedges and 1-irons on the green, and was actually 1-up

before losing the last two holes. Crenshaw's opponent, Eamonn Darcy, even conceded a three-and-a-half-footer on the eighth, apparently because he thought Crenshaw was avoiding his putter on purpose.

The story is entertaining, but it's also poignant. Crenshaw was blessed with such exquisite touch that he believes Little Ben was never the same after the buckeye incident, despite the 25 different shafts he had put on the club and one attempt by a jeweler to solder the two broken pieces together. "I guess I just wish I had Little Ben back the way he was," Crenshaw wrote.

If there's a moral in all of this, it's that you should think twice before swinging your putter at a buckeye, jamming it into your bag, stuffing it in a trash can, throwing it in the lake, leaving it by a watercooler, breaking it over your knee, or putting it in the way of a Simon Hobday practical joke. Just ask some of the best golfers in the world.

It's the Ryder Cup and Ben Crenshaw's putting with a 1-iron—why?
Because he accidentally broke the shaft of Little Ben.

NOW FOR THE GENIUSES

If you're impressed by now at the variety of ways to dump your putter and the imagination some of the world's best golfers have applied to it, please note: they're amateurs. Dilettantes. What follows are three examples of sheer mad genius—although it's not clear whether madness or genius is the prime mover here. Let's just say these guys are good.

And let's start with Lefty Stackhouse, a fine pro between the world wars, who had an explosive temper. He was known to hit his head against a tree after missing a putt. Or he'd slam it against the putter itself. He punched himself once after missing a crucial putt and knocked himself out. (I told you these guys were good.) During one mad outburst, he threw his putter into the water. Of course, it was in his golf bag, so the rest of his clubs hit the water, too. So did his caddy, because Lefty tossed him in as well.

Stackhouse had a contemporary, Ky Laffoon, and they were cast from the same mold. Ky choked his putter once. Another time he dragged it behind his car for 400 miles. Once, at the Sacramento Open, he missed a short one and clubbed his own foot with his putter, breaking the shaft and one of his toes. But don't think the fun was confined to the 1930s. Ky and Lefty have spiritual kin playing on the PGA Tour today. Woody Austin might be one of the circuit's most curious members. He's got a good nature, top-20 talent, and a goofy brain he just can't control. He visited top sports shrink Bob Rotella, and here's what he learned: "When I stand on the golf course, I am the most scared, insecure human being you can imagine," Austin told *Golf Digest*. "I'm a scaredy-cat. I've been to shrinks, sports psychologists, even Dr. Rotella. He's the one who nailed it. I'm one of those people whose brain will not shut off. That's my curse." And at the 1997 MCI Heritage event, Woody went after his own head. In the second round (it's interesting how many putting blowups happen then, when the cut is looming), after leaving a putt about a mile short (a sure sign of bad concentration), he whacked himself over the head five times with the shaft of his putter. A national TV audience got to see it, and Austin got to finish out with his wedge and miss the cut. Later, Austin manfully pointed out he's never torn up the course when he was mad (unlike Tiger Woods) or blamed a fan (unlike Tiger). "If you see me upset, it's going to be directed at myself." And how. To add insult to the injury, Austin was getting gas a few days later in the Buick courtesy car pros get to use at events. The attendant asked him how he was playing, and Austin told him, "Right now, not very well." Replied the attendant: "Hey, you can't be playing any worse than that guy who bent the putter over his head last week!"

Rich Frishman

Woody Austin can make fun of it now, but one afternoon in 1997, he really did try to wrap his putter around his own head. His PGA Tour pals made him this headgear from the actual mangled stick.

Index

NOTE: Italic page numbers indicate photographs